THE SAND AND THE STARS

THE SAND AND THE STARS
The Story of the Jewish People
by DIANA and MEIR GILLON

DECORATIONS BY ANITA BENARDE

VALLENTINE, MITCHELL – LONDON

This edition first published in Great Britain 1975 by
VALLENTINE, MITCHELL & CO. LTD.,
67 Great Russell Street,
London WC1B 3BT

Revised Edition Copyright © 1975 by
DIANA AND MEIR GILLON

ISBN 0 85303 176 2

All rights reserved. No part of this publication may be reproduced, stored in a retrieval system, or transmitted in any form or by any means, electronic, mechanical, photocopying, recording, or otherwise, without the prior permission in writing of the publisher.

Printed in Great Britain

To Scott Meredith,
whose idea it was

CONTENTS

I · The First Jew · 11

II · From Slavery to the Desert · 15

III · Conquest and Exile · 20

IV · Synagogues and Rabbis · 30

V · Jesus · 38

VI · The Jewish Wars Against Rome · 43

VII · The Patriarchate and the Colleges · 53

VIII · Christianity Breaks Away · 58

IX · The Talmud · 63

X · The New Challenge · 72

XI · Jewish Golden Age Under Arabs · 82

XII · Dark Ages in Europe · 92

XIII · Exile From Exile · 100

XIV · Mirages and Havens · 112

XV · Sunrise in the West · 120

XVI · Sunset in the East · 132

XVII · Setback in Western Europe · 139

XVIII · New Trends Among the Jews · 148

XIX · Trends (Continued): Zionism · 160

XX · From Auto-Da-Fé to Gas Chambers · 169

XXI · The Sound of the Messiah's Footsteps · 178

XXII · The Wanderer Goes Home · 191

XXIII · The Diaspora After Hitler · 202

XXIV · The Diaspora After Hitler
Jews in the U.S.A. · 210

XXV · Great Britain · 216

Epilogue · 225

Suggested Reading List · 227

Index · 229

"I will multiply thy seed
as the stars of the heaven,
and as the sand which *is* upon
the sea shore . . ."
Genesis 22, verse 17

In the Talmud, a rabbi explains that these two different similes are in themselves symbolic of the story of the Jews. At times they were to ride as high as the stars. But at other times they would sink as deep as the sand on the shore.

THE FIRST JEW
· I ·

WHAT *is* A JEW? THE WORD IS *Jude* IN GERMAN, *Juif* IN French. All these words are derived from the Hebrew *Yehuda*, or Judah in English.

Judah was the most influential of the twelve ancient Jewish tribes. Each man of that tribe was a *'Yehudi,'* and each woman a *'Yehudit,'* from which comes the English and American name Judith.

Judah was only *one* of the twelve tribes. According to the Bible, Jacob after wrestling with an angel, was given the additional name of Israel, which in Hebrew means "one who has wrestled with an angel." After this the twelve tribes were often called "Israelites." Before that they were called Hebrews, a name that still describes their original language and in some countries is used to refer to them, too, even to this day.

The first meaning of Hebrew—or '*Ivri*—was "across the river." And it was from across the great river Euphrates, from what is today Iraq, that the great-grandfather of Judah, Abraham, first came into the land that has become associated with the Jews. He was the first man recorded to have a vision of one universal God. And to this day those who are converted to Judaism are called, in religious life, "Son— or daughter —of Abraham."

Abraham founded a way of life that developed into what we know now as Judaism. Through it came its two daughter religions: Christianity, which began with Jesus and his disciples nearly two thousand years ago, and Islam, which started with Mohammed in Arabia more than six hundred years later.

Abraham himself was a rich nomad chieftain, who spent his lifetime traveling about the hills and valleys of Canaan, which was later called Palestine. As he moved from oasis to oasis to feed his vast flocks and herds he often found himself opposed by local chieftains who tried to prevent him from getting water. Every time a battle seemed inevitable he must have been doubly terrified, for in his world, every oasis, tribe, village, city, and well had its own special god, which was supposed to protect place and people. And Abraham was a stranger, often away from his own gods.

However, he had to fight, for without water he and

The First Jew

his immense following of retainers and flocks and herds could not survive. Strangely enough, his forces usually won. And because they won, he began to think: If these gods are really all-powerful on their own ground, as people say, how is it possible for my god to win in a strange land? At last it occurred to Abraham that there were no local gods. He had a sudden blinding revelation: There was only one god over all—the Creator of the whole world.

All the same, Abraham was still a creature of his time. He had always taken for granted that all gods had to be kept in a good humor. One had to bribe them to produce rain, cure sickness, chase off locusts, and so on. One had to offer them sacrifices of one kind or another. On really important occasions the sacrifices were of human beings.

To begin with, Abraham thought that his one god was like all the others in this way. So, the Bible says, he built an altar on which he tied down his beloved only son, Isaac, ready for the supreme sacrifice. But as he raised his knife to strike, Abraham had his second revelation. A god who had created the world with man as its most important living creature would surely not wish to have that man deliberately destroyed. So instead of his son he killed a ram, for he still could not imagine a god that required *no* sacrifice. From that day on neither he nor his descendants ever resorted to human sacrifices, except for short periods when they imitated their pagan neighbors.

Faint shadows of early man's belief in sacrifices survive even in our time in almost all societies. In Judaism now, once a year, on the eve of the most solemn of all Jewish fasts, the Day of Atonement, very strict Jews offer the life of a chicken as a token of their own lives. Of course, the chicken is eaten by the family, not burned on any altar. Moslems sacrifice animals on some of their feast days. Christianity made its central theme the onetime sacrifice of Jesus for the whole of humanity, a sacrifice recalled by the symbolic bread and wine in every Communion service.

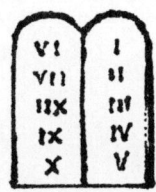

FROM SLAVERY TO
THE DESERT
· II ·

DURING A GREAT FAMINE IN CANAAN, ABRAHAM'S grandson, Jacob-Israel, had moved with all his wives and children and slaves and flocks and herds southwest along the Mediterranean seacoast to Egypt, where there was more food. They settled in the east of the Nile Delta country and their descendants stayed there happily for many generations.

Then, in 1583 B.C., the Hyksos kings of Egypt, who had treated them well, were overthrown. The new king, or pharaoh, looked very suspiciously at the greatly increased and prosperous tribes of Israelites and decided to turn them into slaves. For years they labored, under the whips of overseers, on the building of the great pyramids. A later pharaoh, afraid that in the event of war the Israelites would join his enemies, went so far as to try to destroy them altogether, by ordering the destruction of every newborn male Israelite child.

One of the Israelite women hid her baby until he was three months old. Then she tucked him into a tiny boat of reeds and put it among the tall iris plants at the river's edge. A royal princess found it and rescued the baby. She called him Mosheh, or Moses in English, and he was brought up as a member of the pharaoh's court. When as a young man he came upon an Egyptian attacking an Israelite slave, he went to the slave's rescue and killed the Egyptian in the struggle. To escape punishment he had to leave Egypt. He settled in the Sinai Peninsula, near-desert country, and there he married the daughter of a local priest.

After some years had passed, Moses had a vision that God was ordering him to return and demand from the pharaoh permission for the Israelites to leave Egypt altogether. He went back, but the pharaoh took no notice of his plea "Let my people go." Then, ancient tradition says, God brought down on Egypt one plague after another to warn the pharaoh of what would happen if he did not give in to Moses' demands. The Nile turned red as blood, swarms of locusts devastated every green thing. After each plague the pharaoh promised to let the Israelites go, but changed his mind the next day and became more savage than ever in his attitude.

Finally, there came the tenth plague, an epidemic

From Slavery to the Desert

that attacked Egyptian children. As if by some miracle, Israelite children were unharmed. For, says the story, the Israelites were ordered by Moses to mark the doorways of their houses so that the Angel of Death would "pass over" them.

The pharaoh lost his own child, and at last ordered Moses to take his people away as quickly as possible.

The Israelites departed in great haste, not even allowing time for their bread dough to rise before they baked it. Jews now commemorate this deliverance of their forefathers by eating unleavened bread each year at the Passover feast.

Almost at once the pharaoh changed his mind again, and went off with an army and chariots in hot pursuit of the Israelites to bring them back to slavery. He caught up with them just as they were crossing into the Sinai Peninsula over a marshy arm of the Red Sea, probably near the area where the Suez Canal runs through the Sea of Reeds today. Then "the Lord caused the sea to go back by a strong east wind . . . and made the sea dry land." Moses and his followers "went into the midst of the sea upon the dry ground" (Exodus 14:21–22) and escaped while the pursuing Egyptians were sucked down into the marsh and drowned. "And the water returned, and covered the chariots, and the horsemen, and all the host of Pharaoh that came into the sea after them; there remained not so much as one of them" (Exodus 14:28).

It is one of the great miracle stories of the Old

Testament, the great history and law book that contains the early Jewish story. But it could be explained in practical terms. The heavily armed Egyptians in their metal chariots would have had more difficulty in crossing marshland than the lightly laden Israelites. Besides, the flocks and herds of the fugitives would have churned up the marsh and made it more impenetrable than ever.

According to the Old Testament, the journey from Egypt to Canaan took forty years. Moses did not lead the Israelites along the short coast route. There they would have encountered fierce warrior tribes, and they might have lost heart at the thought of hard fighting. Instead, Moses led them a long way around into the depths of the Sinai desert, going from oasis to oasis, from well to well, teaching them, training them, always with an eye on the young people. In the meantime, too, he sought to restore their faith in the *one* God—a concept that had become dim during the many years among Egypt's myriad idols.

Moses began his teaching with the fundamental laws, the Ten Commandments, a remarkable set of rules for conduct between one man and another.

The Old Testament tells how Moses went up to Mount Sinai and stayed there forty days and forty nights communing with God. Then the Israelites, thinking perhaps that he was not going to return, built themselves a calf of gold and worshiped it. When Moses returned with the stone tablets bearing the Com-

From Slavery to the Desert

mandments and saw what had happened, he was so angry that he smashed the tablets in pieces. Only after the Israelites wholeheartedly repented did he return to the mountaintop and bring back another set.

One of these Commandments introduced a revolutionary idea in the social development of man. This was the decree that "the seventh day is the sabbath," which everyone, including servants and animals, must keep holy by resting from labor. It is difficult for us to realize how extraordinary this idea must have seemed at the time. Even as late as the first century A.D. in ancient Rome poets mocked the Jews for their way of life. Second to the best joke about the invisible Jewish God was this lazy habit of resting every seventh day.

Moses did not merely teach the people to worship the one God. He educated them to the idea that to please God one had to be kind and just to others. This code of behavior became the foundation of Jewish belief, and to this day it is the moral code that most civilized people live by.

CONQUEST AND EXILE
· III ·

IT HAS BEEN CALLED BY DIFFERENT NAMES IN DIFFERENT periods—Canaan, Judah/Israel, Judea, Palestine, and now Israel and Jordan, but that strip of country bordering the eastern Mediterranean Sea has made a deeper mark on the world's history than any of the great empires. Many people think of it as the birthplace or cradle of civilization.

Tiny by European standards, minute by American ones, this land is squashed between the Arabian desert on the east and the Mediterranean on the west. Lebanon lies to the north, Syria to the northeast, the Sinai desert and the Red Sea Gulf of 'Aqaba on the south. It is a kind of southwestern outpost of Asia, jutting between Europe and Africa.

Conquest and Exile

This location has always been both a blessing and a curse to its people. The ancient trading routes, north-south, east-west, crossed the land. With trade went a great exchange of ideas, which was good. But the land was also a corridor for the armies of the great empires on their way to new conquests. More often than not they marched right over the country's inhabitants, crushing them in the process.

The Israelites had been wandering for years before, at last, Moses' scouts, one from each tribe, came back with their report on the Land of Canaan that lay ahead. All twelve of them agreed that the country "flowed with milk and honey." To prove it, they brought back figs, pomegranates, and a bunch of grapes so huge, the Bible says, that it took two men to carry it slung across a pole.

The scouts had done a fairly detailed survey. Talking to the inhabitants of the scattered towns, they must have discovered that the country had an immensely varied climate. Up in the mountains in the winter months it was very cold, so that people had to wear heavy clothes of skins or wool. The houses there were strong and thick-walled, stone-built against not only the heavy winter rains but the cold white storms of snow that came every third or fourth year. In the plains, by the coast, it was hot in summer. Even in winter nobody suffered from the cold, although the heavy rains would turn the fertile soil into a sea of mud.

There were two great lakes. The more northern lake, called Kinneret or the Sea of Galilee, lay below sea level, so that the surrounding country was warm and full of flowers in wintertime. The second lake, more to the south, the Dead or Salt Sea, lay deeper still. Its water was always warm and strangely salty and oily to the touch. Nothing grew in the gray hills surrounding it. There were no fish in its waters. Farther south, on the shores of the Red Sea, rain fell only about ten days in the year.

All these varied climates produced an enormous choice of fruits and vegetables, some unobtainable even in the rich Nile Delta in Egypt. Certainly they were undreamed of in the desert where the Israelites had been wandering for so long.

Just the same, ten of the twelve scouts were strongly against invading Canaan. There was little chance of success, they reported. The country was inhabited by fierce warrior people living in strongly fortified villages. Some of these people were giants, they insisted.

The other two scouts, one of them named Joshua, disagreed. In the end it was these two men who carried the day. With Joshua in command, the Israelites drove into Canaan from the southeast, then crossed the Jordan and worked their way westward, leaving pockets of resistance when they found them too strong. The coastal plain they left alone for the time being, because its inhabitants were too well armed and equipped with chariots. The people on the southern half of the coast were called Philistines. They had originally been sea raiders from the island of Crete and the coasts of Asia

Conquest and Exile

Minor. The northern coastline was settled by the Phoenicians.

So the Israelites settled down mainly in fortified villages and towns in the hills. The twelve tribes were still far from being united; they were held together simply by their common religious beliefs. Each town or village was ruled by its Elders. Only when they were attacked from outside did the tribes unite, under some leader who emerged in the hour of need. These leaders were known as Judges; among the most famous were Deborah in about 1150 B.C. and later Samson, remarkable for his fight against the Philistines.

The last of the Judges was Samuel. As he grew older, and the Philistine attacks became fiercer, the people begged him to appoint a real king.

Samuel warned them against this in a thoroughly republican speech: "If you have a king ruling over you," he said, "he will take your sons and make them drive his chariots and ride his horses, and even run in front of his own chariot. He will turn your daughters into confectioners and cooks and bakers."

In spite of this dismal prospect the people insisted. And, more than a thousand years before the birth of Christ, Saul, a handsome young man from the Tribe of Benjamin, was anointed king by Samuel.

According to the historians who several hundred years later wrote the biblical Book of Samuel, Saul was not such a disastrous tyrant as Samuel had threatened. He was almost a modern "democratic" king, easily accessible to the people, and so were his successors. Occasionally one of them would find power going to his head. Usually, when this happened, some "prophet" would appear to denounce him and remind him that although God had made him king, he was only a man like any other. This was in great contrast to the Oriental despots who ruled all around them.

The ancient Jewish prophets were really the keepers of the people's conscience. In the desert, God had angrily called the Jews a "stiff-necked people." They hated any form of dictatorship. Their prophets were guardians of civil rights, who complained about any injustice, whether it came from high or low. Prophets might turn up anywhere. Sometimes they were aristocrats from the court itself or priests. But just as often they were men of the people—shepherds from the hills or plowmen from the fertile valleys.

Saul was followed by David, who became king over all Israel in 1006 B.C. and far outshone him. He was the youngest son of a well-to-do family from the town of Bethlehem, in the hills a few miles south of Jerusalem, in the territory of the Tribe of Judah. Chosen by Samuel as heir when Saul was still on the throne, David became famous even as a youngster for his defeat of Goliath, the Philistine champion. The shepherd boy with nothing but his slingshot and five pebbles laid low the giant in full armor, bristling with weapons as he stood and mocked his attacker.

Legends grew up around this hero David, who was not only a superb general but also traditionally the author of the Psalms. The Psalms, a magnificent collection of poems, covers almost every possible mood and problem in the spiritual and emotional life of man, from pride in conquest to despair.

David may or may not have written the Psalms, but he was unquestionably a great conqueror. It was he who captured Jerusalem and made it his capital. But when it came to building an altar to God, he did not want to rely on conquest. Like Abraham, who insisted upon paying for the cave and the field at Machpelah for a burying place for his people (Genesis 23), David paid cash in a regular business transaction for the threshing floor of a conquered local chieftain. But he could not build a temple on it because he had a vision of God telling him that he had shed too much blood in his many wars.

It was his son Solomon, when he became king, who raised a magnificent temple on the threshing floor. It was built of great blocks of golden Jerusalem stone and cedar timber from Mount Lebanon in the north. It was ornamented with rich and elaborate carving and plated and inlaid with gold.

In this Temple the hereditary priests, members of the Tribe of Levi, made daily sacrifices of animals while they prayed for the welfare of the nation. But individual people, too, even non-Israelites, could bring their own sacrifices to the priests and make their own prayers, as some people will buy and light a candle in a church today.

Solomon's kingdom was really an empire. It embraced not only the Land of Canaan, including the Philistine territory, but most of Syria in the north.

The Phoenicians on the northern coast with their seaports were left alone. They had been allies of King David, and Solomon made them useful partners in his enterprises. They supplied cedars for the Temple and the palaces, and their expert shipbuilders and seamen served the combined merchant fleets, which traded with Africa and the Far East through the new port, Ezion-geber, that Solomon had built on the Gulf of 'Aqaba.

The Prophet Samuel's warning to the Israelites about the demands a king would make came true with a vengeance under Solomon. His empire required soldiers and horses and chariots; his vast building projects needed laborers. He was always having to raise large sums of money, which meant heavy taxes. The Israelites groaned.

When he died and was succeeded by his son Rehoboam, a deputation from the people demanded cuts in taxation and an all-round loosening of the government's reins. Rehoboam was not at all sympathetic and according to the Bible retorted, "My father chastised you with whips, but I will chastise you with scorpions!" (I Kings 12:14)

Rebellion followed, and in about 930 B.C. all the tribes except Judah and Benjamin broke away and established a separate kingdom, taking in the center and north of the country. It was to be called the

Conquest and Exile

Kingdom of Israel. The southern kingdom of Judah and Benjamin, with Jerusalem as the capital, became known as the Kingdom of Judah.

Unfortunately for the Kingdom of Israel, it lay across the path of conquest of a newly arisen empire, Assyria. After conquering the land in the north, the Assyrians found the Kingdom of Israel in the path of their intended march on Egypt. So, two hundred or so years after the split, in 715 B.C., the Northern Kingdom of Israel fell to Assyria.

From then on it disappears from history. The most important of its inhabitants were taken off by the Assyrians, and what happened to them remains a mystery. Some believe that the Jews of the Caucasus and Kurdistan may be their descendants. Many other groups of people, from the New Zealand Maori to the Beni Israel Jews of India, have at one time or another been thought to be descended from these lost Jews. There is even a sect that believes the British are the "Lost Tribes."

However, the people of the Northern Kingdom were not the first to disappear after being conquered by Assyria. The Assyrian policy was to subjugate a conquered people by deporting the upper classes and the educated element who might encourage rebellion. To make doubly sure, the Assyrians replaced exiles from one country with exiles from another, with no common language or culture between them. Only generations of intermarriage could produce a vigorous new nation.

The Jews who were left in the Northern Kingdom were in no position to develop their religion any further. Their educated classes and leaders had been taken away from them. Their faith, therefore, remained as it was at the time of the Assyrian conquest—the rudimentary early beliefs and laws. The foreign exiles who had been imported by the Assyrians had mixed and intermarried with these Israelites and become assimilated. From here on they were no longer known as Israelites but as Samaritans, after their capital city, Samaria.

The Kingdom of Judah managed to survive about 130 years longer than the Northern Kingdom. It was mostly mountains and desert, and lay off the warring empires' beaten track. Its kings were usually diplomatic enough to stay neutral in the empires' wars.

This isolation helped the Judeans to preserve their beliefs, which were far ahead of anything else in the world at the time. But this tranquility came to an end in 605 B.C. when Assyria itself was conquered by a new power, Babylonia. In advancing on Egypt, Nebuchadnezzar, the Babylonian emperor, invaded the Kingdom of Judah. In 597 B.C. its eighteen-year-old king, Jehoiachim, had to surrender. Nebuchadnezzar thought that he could destroy any tendency to future rebellion by taking with him into Babylonia ten thousand Judean prisoners—the princes and other nobles, the priests and the merchants.

However, it was not long before the Judeans, or Jews as they were beginning to be called, made an alliance

Conquest and Exile

with Egypt against Babylonia. Nebuchadnezzar attacked again. In 586 B.C. his troops looted and destroyed Solomon's Temple and Jerusalem itself. All the inhabitants, except for the peasants, were taken into Babylonia and settled there in the rich fertile province between the Tigris and the Euphrates rivers, which today is called Iraq. Large numbers of their descendants continued to live there until the 1950's.

SYNAGOGUES AND RABBIS
· IV ·

WHEN CONQUEST CAME TO THE SOUTHERN KINGDOM, Judah, its people had had an extra 130 years of independence, during which they were guided by both the Temple priests and the prophets. For most of the time they also had stable governments under wise kings. One of these, Hezekiah, even introduced something like a compulsory education system. There were few illiterates among the Jews from then on.

When exiled from their homes and Temple, they did not go as a spiritually empty people. Their religion was already well developed and so were their laws, customs, and traditions. They had their books with them and they could all read them. But they still felt lost without

Synagogues and Rabbis

Jerusalem and its Temple with which the ritual of their faith was bound up. There, men from all over the country had brought their offerings and annual tax, the half-*shekel*. There they had made their pilgrimages for the three great national festivals, Passover, Pentecost or "First Fruits," and Tabernacles, a kind of Harvest Thanksgiving.

On their sad march from home into exile, and then in their new, strange country, the Judeans had with them one of the greatest of the prophets, Jeremiah. He was not only a prophet, but a member of the priestly family of Kohanim. (Any Jew today called Cohen, Kahn, Cahaan, or Kohn, or even Katz, this last word created from the Hebrew initials of a phrase meaning a true priest, is descended from this family.)

Jeremiah encouraged the exiles to settle down, to sow wheat and barley, to plant vineyards, or, if they lived in cities, to work for their well-being. He taught them also not to forget Jerusalem. "If I forget thee, O Jerusalem," ran a sad ballad of the period, now sometimes sung in the Psalms, "let my right hand forget *her cunning*" (Psalm 137:5).

At the same time Jeremiah persuaded them that their faith was not tied to the stone and mortar of Jerusalem and its glorious Temple, which now lay in ruins. In Babylon, Jeremiah preached that what was important was the spiritual idea of their religion, and this was universal. Jews must remain faithful to their own invisible God, must not slip into local idol worship, and must not forsake the Torah, the Law. (The Torah contained the early books of the Bible, which had been written down about a hundred years earlier.) In this way, Jeremiah laid the foundations of the religion that has united the Jews ever since, even away from their homeland.

Although the exiles no longer needed the Temple to keep them together, they still had to have their spiritual centers. In Babylonia the synagogue, the meetinghouse began. (Synagogue is the Greek word for the Hebrew *k'nesset*, which means "assembly.") The synagogues had no sacrifices or priests. They were simply places where the Babylonian Jews met to pray and to discuss the Law. The accent of the Torah was always on righteousness—that is, justice, kindness, and charity to the poor, and even kindness to animals. These early Babylonian synagogues were not merely the origin of present-day Jewish synagogues. They were also the forerunners of the Christian church and the Moslem mosque.

About fifty years after the Exile, in 538 B.C., Babylonia in its turn was conquered by Persia. The new emperor, Cyrus, allowed all Jews who wished to do so to go back to rebuild Jerusalem and the Temple. Although most of them remained in Babylonia, where they had been born and where they were happy, a few thousand set out on the long trek through the desert back to their parents' homeland.

Arriving there, however, they found not only the people from the Southern Kingdom who had escaped

Synagogues and Rabbis

Nebuchadnezzar's exile, but Samaritans from the north who had moved in and claimed squatters' rights.

This in itself raised no great problems for the returned exiles. But they had a very serious spiritual worry. For these Samaritans practiced a religion that was but a primitive shadow of the Judaism of the Babylonian Jews. Moreover, many of these Samaritan squatters had intermarried so much with the people of neighboring nations that they had incorporated some of the beliefs of the idol worshipers into their own religion.

No wonder that the returned exiles, who had given up the comforts of their settled homes and crossed deserts to rebuild a ruined Jerusalem and Temple, should reject the Samaritan offer to help with the rebuilding. The Samaritans were offended, and they united with other chieftains living in the south, east, and north of the country to hinder the reconstruction work. Their constant raids made the returned exiles work with spade in one hand and sword in the other, as the Bible describes it.

Finally, the Samaritans built a rival shrine on Mount G'rizim, near what is now Nablus, and established their own priesthood. The break became final, and the few hundred surviving Samaritans worship on their holy mountain to this day.

In 515 B.C. the exiles finished rebuilding the Temple, which again became a center for the nation—for sacrifices and pilgrimages. Every town and village built its own synagogue. There, the local man most familiar with the Law, the *rav* or master (*rabbi* simply means "my master"), took charge of daily prayer and the study of the Torah.

About 150 years later Judea came under the rule of a northeastern Mediterranean empire centered in Syria. Its Greek emperor, Antiochus, thought he could make it safe from rebellion by forcing the Greek culture, gods, and way of life on all his subject peoples. The pagans took this without protest. But when Antiochus set up a statue of Jupiter in the Temple at Jerusalem, and sacrificed a pig on the altar, he was inviting rebellion from the Jews.

A band of fiercely pious men, led by a priest named Mattathias the Hasmonean and his five sons, retreated to the caves in the limestone mountains of Judea. From there they made lightning-like guerrilla raids on the Greeks. The most famous of the five brothers was Judah the Maccabee, or "the hammer."

They fought like lions, but they soon found that they were handicapped by their religion. For they had to rest on the Sabbath, and their enemies simply waited until that day to attack, knowing they would meet no resistance. Judah the great warrior then became a religious reformer. He ruled that the preservation of life was more important than the command to observe the Sabbath, and that to save one's life one must fight. The Jews began to win small battles and then greater ones. Little by little they drove the Greeks back and eventually recaptured Jerusalem. Then they cleansed the Temple, rededicated it, and rekindled the eternal lamp on the altar. This the Jews to this day commemorate

Synagogues and Rabbis

by lighting candles on the Feast of Hannukah.

One after another, four of the Maccabee brothers were killed in battles or by assassination. The last brother, Simon, was made High Priest, Prince and Military Commander, the office to be hereditary in his family, proclaimed so by "the great congregation of the priests and people and rulers of the nation and elders of the country."

Unfortunately his descendants did not carry on a democratic tradition. They became increasingly autocratic, caring little for the wishes of the people. The "stiff-necked" Jews, in their resentment of the pompous court and the Temple priesthood that went along with it, came to rely more and more on their rabbis. These were men of the people, unpretentious men who in the evenings and on rest days taught and expounded the Law in the local synagogue. They could be met in ordinary daily life as shoemakers, smiths, and shopkeepers.

Soon the people became divided into two separate sects. The Sadducees, who supported the king and consisted mainly of the aristocracy, the Temple priesthood, and the big landowners were on one sdie, the Pharisees —rabbis and their followers—on the other.

The word Pharisees (the word in Hebrew is *p'rushim*, meaning "dissenters") is one that has crept into English with a meaning very different from its original sense. "Pharisaical" has come to mean over-fussy about the letter of the law, even hypocritical. But it was the Sadducees who were really like that. The Pharisees were reformers, the people who tried to rescue Judaism from the formalism and mummification into which the Sadducees were pressing it. By tactful and careful interpretation, the Pharisees brought in new ideas and adapted Judaism to the new conditions of life.

Some of these Pharisee rabbis interpreted the Law quite broadly. The greatest of them was Rabbi Hillel, the head of a great theological college, whose teachings are still followed by Jews today. There is a story that once a non-Jewish soldier promised Hillel that he would become a Jew if Hillel could tell him the whole of Judaism while he stood on one leg.

"I will tell you," said Hillel. "Do not do to others anything that you would not wish done to yourself."

In this Hillel was expressing the true essence of Judaism, which puts its whole stress on the relationship between man and his fellow men, rather than that between man and God. The annual Day of Atonement (*Yom Kippur*), for instance, consists of a twenty-five hour Fast, spent repenting of sins and praying for forgiveness. But this cannot wipe out sins against fellow human beings. God is merciful; He will forgive sins against Himself—such as eating forbidden foods or breaking the Sabbath. But any injury to another person, such as theft, assault, cheating, can only be forgiven by the injured person himself.

In a way the Sadducee-Pharisee rift was an early class struggle of artisans, peasants, and workers standing for progress against a hereditary priesthood and aristocracy that wanted to keep things as they were.

Synagogues and Rabbis

The quarrel came to a head during the reign of a tyrant king named Alexander Jannai. In the middle of a banquet celebrating one of the king's victories, a Pharisee rabbi stood up and demanded that Alexander give up either his title of king or his religious title of high priest. Sometime later, when the king was officiating as high priest in the Temple during the Feast of Tabernacles, he used the old Sadducee ritual, not the reformed Pharisee one. So the congregation pelted him with their citrons (a large lemon-like fruit that observant Jews carry to prayers during that particular feast). There was a riot, which was put down with much bloodshed. A little later, open rebellion broke out, followed by six years of ferocious civil war. Alexander hired foreign mercenaries and crushed the rebellion. But on his deathbed he advised his queen and successor, Salome Alexandra, who was the sister of a Pharisee leader, to make peace. And for the seven years of her rule peace did reign.

When she was dying, her younger son, helped by the Sadducees, tried to seize the throne. Both he and his brother, the real heir, appealed for help to the Romans, a newly risen power from the West. Pompey, the Roman general, had already conquered Syria, and he was delighted to have an excuse to enlarge the empire. In 63 B.C. he occupied Jerusalem and cut off much of the country's territory altogether. The rest he proclaimed as a Roman province called Judea. Thus the Jews lost their independence again.

JESUS
·V·

ABOUT SIXTY YEARS AFTER JUDEA CAME UNDER ROMAN rule, Jesus was born in Bethlehem, a large village south of Jerusalem. At the time, the king of Judea was Herod the Great, so-called because he became famous for building new cities and theaters dedicated to the Roman emperor not only in his own country but also in Syria and Greece. He also rebuilt the Temple in Jerusalem on a magnificent scale. Herod was the son of a chief of the Edomites in the extreme south of the country, who had been converted to Judaism in Maccabee days. But he himself had married a princess of the Hasmonean Maccabee family.

Aside from his great building work, he was a pitiless tyrant, not just over his subjects but over his own family.

Jesus

At one time or another he had three of his sons executed on suspicion that they had been plotting against him. He also killed his beautiful wife, Miriamne, because Salome, his scheming sister, told him that Miriamne was having a love affair with the Roman general Mark Anthony. The Roman Emperor Augustus remarked once that it was safer to be Herod's pig than his son.

Although the Jews disliked their tyrant king, their real hatred was for their Roman overlords. All the other Roman colonies also resented Rome, but they came, in time, to accept their position as subject peoples. Judea never did. The Jews detested Roman ways and Roman gods. More than anything, they loathed the Roman worship of their emperor as a god.

Rome was a very harsh master. Any hint of rebellion was tracked down by its efficient intelligence service. And convicted rebels died by crucifixion, that cruel Roman punishment. All over the Roman Empire countless numbers perished in that way—slowly, nailed on crosses in the blazing sun or the cold mountain winds.

In their miseries the Jews took hope from the ancient promises of the prophets that one day the Anointed of God, the Messiah, would deliver them from all their enemies. Inevitably this idea had many different interpretations and various sects sprang up. Many of these groups despaired of this world altogether and found comfort only in the Hereafter, where justice and freedom would reign supreme. If life was so apt to end in the gutter or on the cross, the innocent Jewish victims would at least die knowing that their souls would survive, while their wicked heathen persecutors would writhe in eternal damnation. The body did not matter, for anyone could see that it rotted away after death. But the soul was eternal.

Some withdrew from the world when they were still alive. Some sects, like the Essenes, went off into the desert on the shores of the Dead Sea. From the earliest times, in this wild expanse of gray hills and rocks and innumerable caves prophets and other unconventional beings had found refuge and inspiration.

The desert sects founded colonies, where, living by simple communal rules, they spent their days in work, prayer, and meditation. Some historians believe that John the Baptist and later Jesus had been members of one of these sects. Books and copies of parts of the Bible were found in a cave by a wandering Arab shepherd in 1948. Although they had been there for about two thousand years, many of them are still clearly legible. They have become known as the Dead Sea Scrolls. The rolls of parchment had been stored in pottery jars, and the dry air of the mountain desert had preserved them. Very careful study of these books has convinced many scholars that the Dead Sea communities were forerunners of Christianity.

This was the Judea—oppressed, resentful, hopeful, with guerrilla rebels always lurking in the hills, particularly in Galilee—into which Jesus was born and grew up. Like many other brilliant and thoughtful youths, he took part in discussions of the Law with gatherings of grown-up men. Later, like many other young rabbis, he

Jesus

tramped the country discussing his ideas with anyone who was ready to listen.

His followers grew in numbers. But he also made enemies, for his ideas were often revolutionary. He was fighting the current Pharisaic tendency to solidify its teaching into a set of rules as inflexible as the Sadducean laws had been. To Jesus, the Pharisee rabbis seemed to have lost the original fire of liberalism and reform that had inspired them in their early days.

Jesus questioned some of the overstrict rules that had grown up around the Ten Commandments. For instance, the Sabbath rest-day command, a wonderful social idea, had been interpreted by some of the stricter rabbis so that it appeared to Jesus that they had altogether lost sight of the original meaning. According to them, for example, plucking a handful of ripening corn while strolling in a field on the Sabbath was just as forbidden as the hard labor of reaping and threshing. Jesus taught that the Sabbath had been made for man, not man for the Sabbath.

Like the prophets before him, Jesus also preached that the relationship between man and man was more important than empty ceremonial. He also never tired of reminding those who knew that they had done wrong that they were not eternally damned. There was still time to repent and determine to do good in the future.

More and more followers flocked after him. Almost all of them, of course, including his close friends the Apostles, were Jews, although an occasional Roman did take an interest. These people loved and adored him.

And some of the more nationalistic followers actually began to refer to him as the Messiah they had been waiting for—and even as "King of the Jews." Roman intelligence agents seized on this. Any nationalist movement in a subject people had to be crushed quickly before it could spread.

The tyrannical Romans, of course, had no need of the approval of the Jewish leaders before punishing the rebels, or even the suspects. Life was cheap, and many Jewish rebels had been crucified before.

This time there was a difference, however. Jesus had not preached rebellion. He was the leader of a religious reform movement. But to many of his followers he was the Messiah who would deliver them from the Romans. Such faith, the Romans knew, might erupt into violence at any moment.

The Romans believed that they could nip the movement in the bud by removing its leader. Nonetheless, for appearances sake, it would be wise if the Jewish leaders could be persuaded to cooperate. They, on their part, also feared that if the idea of Jesus as Messiah spread too far, open rebellion would follow, and against all-powerful Rome this could only bring disaster for the entire Jewish people.

Thus Jesus was crucified. It was one crucifixion among thousands, before and after, in Judea and throughout the empire. While we know little or nothing about the others, the crucifixion of Jesus affects the lives of a large part of mankind to this day, nearly two thousand years later.

THE JEWISH WARS AGAINST ROME
· VI ·

THE JEWS CONTINUED TO BE REBELLIOUS. ROME THEN adopted a new policy of tactfulness and greater understanding of the Jews' religious sensitivity. Jewish puritanism about the invisible God had become so fierce as to interpret any display of "graven images" as idolworship. In keeping with the new Roman policy, the governor who had sentenced Jesus, Pontius Pilate, made the concession of removing the imperial images from the governor's palace. When Roman troops marched through Jerusalem, they did not carry their regimental emblems, the eagles, and the statues of the emperor, which they normally bore triumphantly before them.

These new tactics and the removal later of Pontius Pilate because of the many complaints against him, produced a period of quiet in the country. But it did not last. During this time none of the Roman emperors ruled for very long, many of them being cut down by assassins. Provincial governors succeeded one another even faster.

From A.D. 44 there was a series of governors in Judea, ruling for short periods, who showed little consideration for Jewish religious feelings. This produced riots, which in turn led to tyrannical suppression, which only caused more rebellion. In Galilee, a Jewish group called the Zealots became increasingly active. Another even more extreme terrorist group sprang up which assassinated collaborators and sympathizers of the Romans. Its members would mingle with crowds in the towns, stab their victims, and vanish in the confusion. Once they even killed a high priest in this way, in the middle of Jerusalem.

In A.D. 64 a new Roman governor, Florus, arrived. He was even keener on getting rich quickly than his predecessors. He found the country seething with trouble and put down continuing riots and demonstrations with massacres. Two years later, in A.D. 66, he raided the Temple treasury and seized a large quantity of gold.

At this the city rioted. One cynical Jerusalem citizen passed round a basket, begging for coins for the starving Roman governor. This infuriated Florus even more than the riots, and he sent his troops into the city to murder everyone in sight.

The riots only increased and spread further. Florus

sent for reinforcements, and the high priest did his best to calm the people down. But the rebels seized the Temple Mount and forced the Roman legionaries to withdraw to the Jerusalem Citadel. The Jewish puppet king, Agrippa, in Alexandria, Egypt, at the time, hurried back to Jerusalem to try to make peace. But the rebels chased him out of the city.

Eleazar, the son of the high priest and captain of the Temple Guard, persuaded the other priests to stop offering the regular daily sacrifice that was made in the name of the emperor and accompanied by prayers for his well-being.

This was the final signal for general rebellion. But the moderates in Jerusalem appealed for help from the Romans and Agrippa, claiming that the majority of the people remained loyal to Rome. Reinforcements arrived and occupied the upper part of the city, and fighting went on between them and the rebels up and down the steep, narrow streets. Little by little the rebels drove back their opponents, who eventually took refuge in Herod's palace. After a siege, the rebels occupied it, allowing Agrippa's troops and all the other Jewish moderates to leave after they had laid down their arms. But the Roman troops were killed to the last man.

In the meantime a force of rebels had seized Masada, a palace-fortress that Herod the Great had built on a flat twenty-three-acre plateau above sheer cliffs overlooking the Dead Sea. Herod had planned to use it as a refuge against a possible rebellion by his subjects, and also against Cleopatra, queen of Egypt, who coveted

Judea. Now the Jewish rebels killed the entire Roman garrison and occupied the fortress.

From Judea in the south to Galilee in the north, Romans and Jews fought savagely, without mercy on either side. The Roman imperial legate in Syria came down with thirty thousand troops but had to withdraw because winter was coming on. On their retreat to the plains, this force was ambushed in a gorge, losing six thousand men and the equipment of the entire expedition.

This was one of the greatest defeats suffered by a Roman army since the beginning of the empire. It also happened to take place on the historic spot where Joshua, one of Jewish history's greatest generals, had had a miraculous victory more than a thousand years before. The rebels were bound to take this as a good omen, and even the moderates and the "peace party" began to waver.

The Jewish revolutionary authorities were overjoyed and minted new coins to celebrate the new freedom. But after the excitement came the sober awakening. They realized that the mighty Roman Empire would have to save face and wipe out this terrible insult, no matter how much it cost. Otherwise, all the conquered peoples of the empire would rebel. There could be no question now of a negotiated peace.

The Jews knew that time was running out. Soon the Roman war machine would be concentrated on crushing this troublesome outpost that refused to know when it was beaten. The Jews took advantage of the winter, when a Roman attack was unlikely because of the cold

The Jewish Wars Against Rome

and the heavy rains, to organize the country on a wartime footing. But their efforts were amateurish and there was not enough time now to turn a mass of untrained Jews into an organized, effective citizens' army. Even the district commanders were appointed for political rather than military reasons. The Jews had no generals, only fierce guerrilla group leaders.

Joseph ben Mattathias, a member of an aristocratic priest-family, was sent out as commander of the northern province of Galilee merely because he had spent time in Rome and knew something about Roman ways. John of Gishala, a fierce guerrilla leader and a Galilean himself, was bound to oppose the appointment. In Jerusalem itself the appointment of Eleazar, the son of the high priest, as commander was the signal for the beginning of a fierce civil war between Eleazar's supporters and the guerrillas commanded by Simon bar Giora and assisted by the Edomites.

Meanwhile, the Romans had not been wasting time. They brought back Vespasian, one of their best generals, who had been busy subduing the rebellious Britons. With his son Titus, he spent the winter in Syria assembling a huge army. It included not only the best regular Roman legions, but a large force of troops contributed by rulers from all over the empire, from the Britons in the West to King Agrippa himself.

In the spring of A.D. 67 the Romans marched south from Syria into Galilee. Joseph ben Mattathias, after some courageous fighting, surrendered—and actually joined the Romans. Vespasian was recalled to Rome to succeed the mad Emperor Nero, who had committed suicide. Titus became commander-in-chief of all the forces in Judea, and Joseph ben Mattathias became his friend and adviser. Later Joseph settled in Rome as a member of Vespasian's court, and was appointed official historian, with a salary from the emperor himself. It is as a historian that he is known today, under his Roman name of Flavius Josephus. Although Josephus has ever since been regarded by Jews as an arch-traitor, his *History* remains a magnificent source of detailed information on the period, even though it has an obvious pro-Roman slant.

After the fall of Galilee, those who wanted to continue the struggle, led by John of Gishala, fled to Jerusalem. There they added to the confused internal fighting for control between Eleazar and Simon bar Giora.

Simon stood for the people against the middle classes. He was an extreme revolutionary, even to the extent of liberating the slaves—at a period when slaves were the foundation of every country's economy. In the fierce fighting the Jerusalem grain stores went up in flames, bringing starvation to the besieged citizens and the thousands of refugees from Roman-occupied territory. According to Josephus, more people died inside Jerusalem from starvation and internal fighting than were killed by the Romans.

Finally, on the tenth day of May A.D. 70 Titus with his huge army began the siege of Jerusalem itself. The Jews inside stopped quarreling and closed their ranks against the enemy at the gates. The city was surrounded by three concentric walls, and there were many underground passages through the limestone caves beneath. Now and then, the Jews would open the gates and send out squads to attack the Romans. Or raiding parties would use the underground passages to make surprise attacks on the Roman siege engines and set them on fire. These engines were huge towers of timber, from which big mechanical slingshots called *ballistae* hurled enormous rocks into the besieged city. The towers were also armed with great iron horns, which were rammed into the wall in front until it gave way.

Nonetheless, the Jews had wasted too much valuable manpower, time, and food, and they were fighting the world's most efficient army. According to Josephus, Titus himself approached the wall on one occasion and pleaded with the defenders to surrender and save the city and themselves. No doubt he wanted to preserve the Temple, the most famous shrine in the eastern half of his father's empire. But the Jews refused to give in.

The Romans breached one wall after another. The battle continued to rage until August 29, the ninth day of the Jewish month of Av, when the Romans broke into the Temple area itself and set the Temple on fire. By tradition it was the anniversary of Nebuchadnezzar's destruction of Solomon's earlier Temple, and the date remains a Jewish fast day. The Jews went on fighting, house by house, street by street, with pockets of resisters holding out until September 26.

Titus collected all the treasure he could save from

the Temple fire and carried it off to Rome. With it he took many of the captured Jewish commanders, who later died in the Roman Arena fighting lions, or as gladiators. Many thousands of other prisoners were sold as slaves. The Arch of Titus, which still stands in Rome today, is decorated with carvings of the Jewish prisoners carrying the Temple treasures. Vespasian had coins struck showing captive Jews under a palm tree, and inscribed with the Latin words for "captive Judea."

However, outside Jerusalem, three rebel fortresses still held out. Eventually the Romans captured two; the third, Masada, continued to resist. There were only 967 men, women, and children inside it. Employing a great many slaves and conscripted local people, the Romans succeeded in building a vast ramp of rock and earth to the top of the fortress's walls. On it they erected a ninety-foot-tower with ironclad sides. From its top, under a hail of arrows, spears, and boiling oil thrown from the walls, Roman soldiers worked their siege engines.

When, on the sixteenth of April A.D. 73, the victorious Romans at last clambered over the shattered walls, they expected fierce hand-to-hand fighting. The deathly silence within the walls amazed them. The Jews had first set fire to the building and then committed mass suicide, the men killing their wives and children and then each other. There were only three survivors, two women and a child, who came trembling out of an empty water reservoir where they had been hiding.

The Jewish Wars Against Rome

The great ramp the Romans built and their camps carefully marked out with stones are still visible. When the fortifications of Masada itself were excavated by an international expedition in the 1960's, everything was found as Josephus described it. In addition to skeletons, charred sandals, scrolls, coins, make-up jars, and a woman's long hair, the archaeologists found even the fragments of the pottery that the defenders had apparently used to draw lots for the last man to kill his remaining companions. One of these fragments had on it the name of the leader.

The Romans thought they had settled the Jewish trouble at last. But the messianic fire had not burned out. Jews still believed that God was on their side and would help them if they helped themselves. In A.D. 115 the Jewish communities in Egypt, Libya, Cyprus, and all over the Middle East rose in rebellion against the Emperor Trajan. In A.D. 132 another great rebellion developed in Judea itself against Trajan's successor, Hadrian. It was led by Simon bar Kochba (Son of a Star) and supported by Akiba, the leading rabbi of the time.

At first it met with success. The rebels recaptured Jerusalem, struck coins to celebrate the event, and also made plans to rebuild the Temple. Again the Romans fell back on a great general, Julius Severus, who had to be recalled from settling more trouble in Britain, although the ultimate command was kept by Hadrian himself. Steadily and methodically the Romans pushed on, killing and burning. In A.D. 135, again on the disastrous ninth of Av, the last Jewish stronghold fell.

Simon bar Kochba himself had been killed in the fighting, but the surviving rebels were hunted down and put to death. Rabbi Akiba, then aged over ninety, is said to have been skinned alive. Many thousands of Jews were sold as slaves all over the empire.

The three-year war had been so bitter and destructive that when Hadrian reported his eventual victory to the Roman Senate he omitted the usual formula "I and my army are well."

Determined to leave no ember of possible rebellion, Hadrian decided to fight the Jews by destroying Judaism. All religious practices, from circumcision to the study of the Law, became punishable by death. The city of Jerusalem was literally pulled down, except for the Western Wall of Herod's Temple. There the Romans built a new city, which they called Aelia Capitolina, and a temple dedicated to the Roman god Jupiter. It was a capital offense for any Jew to enter the city, except once a year, when they were allowed to mourn beside the huge stone blocks of the Western Wall. (This afterward became known popularly as the "Wailing Wall.") Even the country's name—Judea—was abolished. To demonstrate that there was no longer any connection between the country and the Jews, Hadrian renamed it Palaestina, after the Philistines, who had once lived in part of the coastal plains. He was sure now that the fierce spirit of Jewish independence had been crushed forever.

THE PATRIARCHATE AND THE COLLEGES
·VII·

DURING TITUS' SIEGE OF JERUSALEM, IN ABOUT A.D. 68, a great rabbi named Yohanan ben Zakkai (*Yohanan* is the Hebrew word from which all Johns, Johanns, Ians, Jans, and so on derive) is supposed to have been smuggled out hidden in a coffin. Titus allowed him to settle in one of the coastal towns. There Yohanan ben Zakkai established a college for the study of Judaism. He also set up a new *Sanhedrin*, or Supreme Jewish Court. Its members were now qualified by their scholarship rather than by political influence and power, as in the past.

Yohanan ben Zakkai taught that justice and righteousness, the fundamentals of the Jewish religion, could be practiced by any Jewish community and did not depend on the Temple. Thus he built a little higher on the solid foundation that Jeremiah had laid centuries before. This was to be the beginning of the lifeline that was to sustain his people through a double catastrophe—the loss of independence and the destruction of the Second Temple.

The disappearance of the Temple also had an unintended effect—the greatest revolution in Judaism since Abraham. The first patriarch had abolished human sacrifice. From A.D. 70, there were to be no animal sacrifices either, because these had been permitted only in the Temple. And now the rabbis, though continuing to teach the laws governing sacrifice, stressed more than ever the message of the ancient prophets that kindness and fairness were more welcome to God than "burnt offerings."

Voluntarily, the Jews set aside a tenth of their income for the upkeep of the colleges, welfare offices, and other institutions. This, of course, was in addition to the heavy taxes they already had to pay to Rome. Again voluntarily, they had their disputes decided by Jewish courts. More than ever the local synagogues, with their magnificent schools for the children and their welfare centers, became the real national focus. All of them worked under the supreme authority of the colleges and the Sanhedrin.

The head of the Sanhedrin was far from being a king, but he was recognized even by the Roman author-

The Patriarchate and the Colleges

ities as Patriarch, or "Prince of the Jews." In theory, he had jurisdiction over the Jews of the whole empire, and the yearly half-*shekel*, originally sent to the Temple, was now given to help the Patriarchate's welfare and educational work.

Most of the centers of learning were in the north, in Galilee. Here, under the Patriarch Judah in the early third century A.D., the rabbis codified all the previous thousands of written and spoken additions to the laws. The work they produced, which was written in clear, concise Hebrew, is known as the Mishnah—the "teaching" or "repetition." But as Judaism came to embrace every second of a Jew's waking hours, in order to survive at all the books of teaching had to alter as life progressed. The Mishnah was a code, but it was not final. It remained open to discussion.

The Palestinian Jews had managed to adjust their religious life to the new conditions. Even economically they tried to put the pieces together. But the population had been drastically reduced by the Simon bar Kochba war. Scores of thousands had been killed in the fighting and in the massacres after the surrender. Hundreds of thousands more had been carried off to be sold as slaves all over the Roman Empire. Many more thousands had fled the country.

Almost wherever they went they found a settled Jewish community ready to give them a helping hand —to ransom slaves, to help the almost penniless immigrants to settle in the new country. For centuries, even before the destruction of the first Temple, adventurous Jews had been traveling outside Palestine. Jewish merchants, like their Syrian and Greek counterparts, had gone overseas in search of trade as far west, some people think, as Cornwall in Britain, and as far east as India and even beyond. Solomon's ships had brought in gold and ivory and apes and peacocks from the Far East and Africa through his port on the Gulf of 'Aqaba, the northern arm of the Red Sea. Many of these traders and merchants remained to settle.

And there were also many thousands of permanent settlers who were not merchants. Some of the exiled Ten Tribes must have continued to practice their religion. Most of the Two Tribes, Judah and Benjamin, did not return home from Babylonia, but stayed there in large and prosperous communities.

By the time of Jesus, there were at least as many Jews outside Palestine as there were inside. Jews lived in Greece, in the Crimea (now in southern Russia), and in various parts of Western Europe. In Rome itself, as many as eight thousand adult Jews signed a petition to the emperor to depose the hated king Herod the Great. More than a third of the inhabitants of Alexandria, Egypt, then the greatest Mediterranean port and cultural center, were Jews.

Everywhere these people were active missionaries for their religion, eager to share the true light with their pagan neighbors. It was a highly sophisticated period—large numbers of intelligent and thinking peo-

The Patriarchate and the Colleges

ple turned away from pagan gods and worship and looked for something to fill the gap. And next door they found the Jews, whose religion taught a clean, honest, and decent life.

Many of these people, from all classes, and even from the emperor's court itself, adopted Judaism completely. Many more found such things as circumcision and the complicated dietary laws too much to accept, and instead became half-Jews—they gave up their idols, observed the Jewish Sabbath, and attended the synagogue meetings.

In fact, in Rome itself, before it became officially Christian, Judaism was a *religio licita*, or a permitted religion, and Jews were exempted from appearing in the law courts on the Sabbath and from taking public office, which involved sacrificing to the Roman gods. (Oddly enough, the Romans called Judaism "atheism" —"no gods"—that is, no *Roman* gods.)

Until about the second century A.D., everywhere in the empire the Jews enjoyed full citizenship rights. Their contacts with Jews in all lands made them particularly successful traders. But everywhere in the empire the Jews were Roman citizens, enjoying full citizenship rights. Because of their contacts with Jewish communities all over the empire, they were particularly successful as traders. But there were Jews in every occupation and profession, even the army.

CHRISTIANITY BREAKS AWAY
· VIII ·

ACTIVE JEWISH MISSIONARY WORK AMONG THE PAGANS was also, naturally enough, taken up by the small, new Jewish sect, the followers of Jesus, for they were as keen as the Pharisees to spread their own version of Judaism. In the first century A.D. Christianity was the latest-comer among the Jewish sects. The Acts of the Apostles, in the New Testament, tells how Paul, a Pharisee Jew before he joined the new sect, usually preached Christianity in synagogues during his missionary journeys outside Palestine.

But it was Paul who planted the seed of the final separation of Christianity from Judaism. In his travels he soon found that the strict demands of Judaism

Christianity Breaks Away

frightened off many would-be converts. A new sort of religious sect was coming into existence, the part-time Jews, who were neither Jews nor pagans.

Paul knew the Jewish laws—the rules about food, the Sabbath, the sacrifices, and so on—but he was deeply convinced that the essentials of Judaism did not lie in the ceremonials, the rituals, and the traditions. He totally identified himself with the early prophets and with Jesus. He went even further than Jesus in readiness to do away with all ritual. Paul did not just preach disregard for the irksome details of the Law. He fervently believed that it was necessary to rescue the world from its idol worship and the disregard for humanity that went with it. These pagan beliefs would be replaced by belief in the *one* and only God and by justice and honesty between men.

Paul went tirelessly from town to town, preaching to the pagans that all that was required of them was faith in Jesus and in his righteous living—to be good and honorable human beings. And thousands who heard him—Jews, part-time Jews, and pagans—flocked to his banner. Soon it was hundreds of thousands.

While Paul's message appealed to the converts, it was utterly repugnant to traditional Judaism, which insisted on observance of the laws and ceremonial ritual. The division between the traditional Jews and the Christian Jews had turned into a break. It grew wider when Emperor Hadrian outlawed the practice of Judaism in A.D. 135. Then it was only natural for the Christians to emphasize the differences between themselves and the Jews and to minimize any resemblance. That same year for the first time they appointed a Gentile, not a Jewish-born Christian, as their bishop of Aelia Capitolina, the new Roman city built on the site of Jerusalem. His predecessors had all been Jewish-born.

From then on the separation of Christian Jews and Pharisee Jews became complete. Each sect fiercely believing that theirs was the only true faith, Jews and Christians argued, quarreled, and sometimes even came to blows. The immediate results were appalling, and none of the early Christians, least of all the Apostles, could have imagined the eventual catastrophe. For in the coming centuries, well into the twentieth, the Jews suffered at the hands of their Christian rulers as no other people had ever suffered before.

The real trouble sprang from the fact that the Christians came to look on themselves as the only true Jews. For they believed that Jews who refused to accept Jesus as the promised Messiah, God's Anointed One, had abandoned their true religion. Therefore, they deserved the Old Testament curses on "those who did evil in the sight of the Lord." On the other hand, they, the followers of Jesus, had kept faith with the prophets who had promised a Messiah. Therefore, *they* were God's truly "Chosen People," entitled to all the blessings promised in the Old Testament.

As the years passed, the story of what led to the

Christianity Breaks Away

crucifixion of Jesus became ever more blurred, ever more prejudiced. Christian writers, still trying to find additional proof that Christianity and the New Testament were the only rightful heirs of the Old Testament and Judaism and that the Jews were accursed heretics, came up with a new argument. They declared that the Jews were not simply nonbelievers in the Messiah—they had actually killed him. They were, therefore, "God killers," to be condemned to eternal damnation.

The chasm between the two religions was further widened in A.D. 325 when the church council of Nicaea went so far as to move the Sabbath from Saturday to Sunday so as to prevent any confusion between them. Before that, Christians had still kept the Jewish Sabbath and the Jewish holy days. The final, unbridgeable gap came during the reign of Emperor Constantine the Great, who favored Christianity and in A.D. 337 became a Christian himself.

Gradually the Christians had gained strength until, from a tiny, weak community, often actually persecuted, they became dominant in the mightiest empire on earth. To the church fathers this was a sign from God that the Christians were His Chosen People. Yet the Jews still refused to see this, still rejected Jesus as their Messiah.

From then on the Christian church councils made one ruling after another that had the effect of suppressing Judaism. Under pagan Rome, the Jews' religion had been called "distinguished"—"certainly permissible." Now the church declarations called the Jews "a nefarious sect" and their synagogue services "sacrilegious gatherings." Another declaration prohibited marriage between Jews and Christians. Finally, Jews were forbidden to own slaves, pagan or Christian, to reduce the risk of anyone falling under Jewish influence. Since Roman culture used slaves much as this century uses buses and telephones and electricity, to forbid slaves to anyone was rather like forbidding public services to people today.

Emperor Theodosius II, who ruled from 408 to 450, placed further restrictions on the Jews. Formulated in A.D. 438, his general Code of Law, the "Roman Law" which is the basis of the laws of all Christian countries, included all existing anti-Jewish laws. It became the blueprint for all laws against the Jews in the future, including, eventually, those laws in Hitler's Germany.

THE TALMUD
·IX·

THE POWER AND AUTHORITY OF CHRISTIANTY WERE growing from strength to strength. There were new converts by the hundreds of thousands, and the reins of government were in Christian hands. In this respect, Judaism was becoming rapidly weaker. Conversion to it was forbidden by law, and Judaism had not only lost its independence in Palestine but had fallen under the harsh control of its greatest rival, Christianity.

However, on another level, the very important one of the development of laws of conduct, Judaism was at an advantage. Christianity's rise to the top had had one inevitable drawback. Its first enormous appeal, that of simplicity, of having discarded a body of complicated

Jewish laws, was bound to wear off. No organization of human beings can exist without fundamental rules, and the church fathers soon found that simple belief in Jesus and decent living were not enough in a world where even saints differed about the definitions of everything. The very belief in Jesus as the Messiah, the Son of God, had to be interpreted, and the thousands of converts from different nations, with their varied cultural backgrounds all had their different versions. This burning sincerity led first to arguments, then to violence, and eventually even to massacres.

In this, at least, the Jews had the advantage. Judaism was sailing stormy oceans, but it had a stout ship, manned by well-trained and like-minded sailors. There was no need to argue about the nature of the Jewish God. He was pure spirit, and unimaginable, and therefore there was nothing to discuss. As for conduct in daily life, expert rabbis were busily adapting past laws to new circumstances as these arose.

The Patriarchate in Palestine continued to develop under the undisputed new aristocracy—the rabbis. Nevertheless, they were discouraged from making scholarship their livelihood. A regular occupation was usual—"without flour there can be no learning" and "the Law must not be made a spade wherewith to dig" were popular sayings. Joshua ben Hanania, for instance, one of the leading rabbis of the time, who had been a Temple singer in his youth, became a blacksmith.

The Talmud

Men like him devoted their studies to the further development of Judaism as they found it—the already codified Mishnah. New cases not dealt with by this code came up before the Jewish courts daily, and judgments had to be pronounced on them. So the rabbis used analogy—similarity to existing laws—or further interpretation of the Old Testament to help them arrive at just decisions.

But their work was not limited to new cases. They went on to introduce entirely new rules, what they called "fences around the law," designed purely to ensure that an existing law could not be broken accidentally. For instance, it was forbidden to eat an animal that had died of disease. The rabbis carried this law further by forbidding the killing of sick animals for food. This meant deciding which animal illnesses were dangerous to human beings. Again, the Jewish day consists of a night and its following day. Many Jews would go on working in their fields and workshops on Fridays until it was quite dark before they began their rest day, the Sabbath. The next day they would start work again as soon as the sun began to sink. Thus hours of the Sabbath could be lost, and this was particularly unfair to servants and slaves. So the rabbis ruled that the Sabbath should begin just *before* sunset and end only when it was dark enough to see three stars.

The codified Mishnah went on developing until there were so many new laws that the additions themselves needed codifying. A beginning was made on this in the year 279, and by the end of the fourth century all the sections dealing with civil law had been edited. This work is called the Palestinian Talmud, Talmud being another Hebrew word for "teaching."

The Talmud is not just Law and Commentaries. It is also full of stories, even of what can only be described as wisecracks. It contains perhaps the earliest written record of the irony for which Jews have become so famous: "Even when God punished the Jews by scattering them," it quotes from a rabbi, "he took care to disperse them all over the world. So when some wicked man wanted to wipe out the Jews in his kingdom, there would still be safety in another."

This was proved again and again in the course of Jewish history. The Jewish people, living by the laws of Judaism, could always survive somewhere. In Palestine Jewish life under Christian Roman government became more and more difficult, so that learning and intellectual life declined. Fortunately, this coincided with the prosperity of the Jews in Mesopotamia (as Babylonia was called by the Greeks and Romans), which was not under Christian rule.

The ancestors of the Mesopotamian Jews had been driven there after Nebuchadnezzar's destruction of the first Temple in 586 B.C. But they still called themselves the *Golah*—"the exile." They were the descendants of those exiles who had preferred to stay when Cyrus of Persia gave permission for the return to Jerusalem. Yet they remained true to their religion and never lost contact with the Palestinian Jews. Their loyalty to the

The Talmud

Jerusalem Temple was unshakable. Every year their voluntary half-*shekels* and other gifts were escorted there by thousands of pilgrims. Those from the priest-families often stayed on in Jerusalem for longer periods to serve in the Temple; one of these even became high priest.

Many of these Mesopotamian Jews were merchants, but the majority were farmers. Archaeologists have found clay tablets of the fifth century B.C. that list Jewish farmers and craftsmen who were either witnesses or parties in the business of a Babylonian bank. As respected members of society, they had a good deal of influence and often made converts among their neighbors, just as the Jews did in the Roman West. In about A.D. 20, the royal family of a small Mesopotamian state on the Tigris River, called Adiabene, embraced Judaism. Its queen, Helena, became so pious that she and some of her family were buried in the Tombs of the Kings outside Jerusalem. And during the Jewish War against Rome of A.D. 66–73, the king of Adiabene sent soldiers to fight for the Jews.

In many ways the Mesopotaman Jews had a great deal of independence. Their Prince of the Exile, or "Exilarch," who was supposed always to be a descendant of David, kept an almost royal state and was recognized and respected by the king as chief of the Jews. The Jews were allowed their own law courts for dealing with internal disputes and could enforce their judgments.

They also established a number of colleges for

the study of the Law. Two of these, at Sura and Pumbeditha, became as well known throughout the Jewish world of the time as Oxford is today. The heads of these two colleges were as important and influential among Jews as the archbishops of Canterbury and York were among the medieval English.

As in Palestine, there were no professional scholars. Before or after a hard day's work in the fields or the shoemaker's shop or the pottery, every man felt it both a duty and a privilege to attend lectures and discussion groups at the nearest synagogue or college. Twice a year, in spring and autumn, when there was less work in the fields, the farmers took a month off to study full time.

It was, therefore, quite natural that the center of Jewish studies should shift eastward when the Patriarchate in Palestine and its own colleges began to decline. And when, in 429, the Patriarchate was abolished altogether by the Christian emperor, and work on the Palestinian Talmud came to an end, the Mesopotamian rabbis and their colleges became the chief authority. Most Jewish communities throughout the world began to follow unquestioningly their pronouncements on the Law.

The accumulation of cases, problems, and interpretations that had gathered during the years soon became a labyrinth in which both rabbis and students were lost. So again a process of sifting and classifying became necessary. Rabbi Ashi worked on this from 375-427,

The Talmud

separating all the available material into different sections. Rabbina II, working from 474 to 499 finished the task by putting everything down in writing, divided into volumes and classified according to subject matter. The language used was the local Aramaic, not its sister-tongue Hebrew, which was now becoming a purely ritual language, used chiefly for prayer.

This collection of books is what we know as the Babylonian Talmud or sometimes *Gemara*. It became the foundation of Jewish life wherever it was lived. The Old Testament itself was no longer enough, even with the additions and interpretations of the Palestinian Mishnah. The lives of all faithful and dutiful Jews could only be directed by the Talmud, with its innumerable additions and interpretations.

One Jewish sect, however, broke away and refused to follow this new rabbinic code. Like the Samaritans or the Sadducees before them, but with some variations, they insisted that the Law as given in the first five books of the Old Testament must not be added to, altered, or interpreted. These people were called the Karaites—"followers of the written word"—and small communities of them still exist.

But the fate of a people without a country of their own, dispersed all over the world, everywhere exposed as small minorities at the mercy of their rulers, eventually caught up with the Jews in Mesopotamia. There came an age of extreme religious intolerance. Territories were constantly being lost, recaptured, and lost again by the eastern half of the Roman Empire, Byzantium, and the Persian Empire. They had been at war on and off for centuries, but since the reign of Constantine, the Byzantine Christians had been fighting a new kind of war. It was no longer merely a question of another town or piece of land or another few hundred thousands of tribute-paying subjects. Now they were fighting for the glory of their young faith. They were out to make the entire world accept Christianity. In these circumstances, toleration of other beliefs and religions was unthinkable.

The pagan Persians, too, caught the infection. If religion was so important to the Christians, it must be powerful, and they, too, began to think in terms of faith as well as territory. Soon it was not enough to capture a new town. Its people must accept the conqueror's religion or suffer.

Yazdegerd II, king of Persia from 440 to 457, in his enthusiasm for Persian Zoroastrianism, tried to suppress Judaism throughout his empire and went so far as to forbid Jews to observe the Sabbath. Under his successor, half of the Ispahan Jewish community, in Persia proper, was slaughtered because of an accusation that they had skinned alive two Zoroastrian priests. The community's children were taken away and forcibly converted. This produced a great flight of Jews from Mesopotamia. The Jews of Malabar, on the coast of Madras, India, may be descendants of some of these refugees.

The Talmud

Twenty years of comparative peace followed this king's death. Then, at the beginning of the sixth century, Kobad, a new Persian ruler, adopted a new religion called Zendicism, which was said to have advocated the sharing of all property, including wives. The Jewish Exilarch Mar Zutra II, supported by some of the non-Jewish population, rebelled. And for seven years he succeeded in maintaining independence in a small area near present-day Baghdad. Eventually, in 520, the rebellion was crushed and Mar Zutra was crucified.

Later Persian rulers were on the whole more tolerant. But these persecutions meant the end of the golden age of Mesopotamian Jewry, although its influence on Jews in other areas continued for some time.

THE NEW CHALLENGE
· X ·

THE JEWS PAID DEARLY FOR THEIR PASSIONATE DEVOtion to the ideas of one God and justice between man and man. Nobody will ever know what would have happened if they had been content to keep these ideas to themselves. If the Jews had not proselytized, would the world perhaps have left them alone?

The historical fact is that they were too eager to share their own blessings with the rest of humanity. In this they succeeded so well that a very large section of humanity came to accept the idea of a universal God. And justice between men is a much desired goal of civilization today.

Their very success led the Jews to disaster after

The New Challenge

disaster. In the West, they had converted the Romans and the Greeks, the majority of whom had adopted the new version of Judaism, Christianity. With the fanaticism of all converts to a new belief, the Christians were determined to establish theirs as the only true religion. The results were catastrophic to the traditional Jews physically although not to the ideas of Judaism itself.

History repeated itself in the East. The Jews in Arabia were equally successful in their enthusiastic missionary work. And again, at the height of their success, six centuries after the birth of Jesus, they were thrown into another caldron of disaster.

Arabia is a vast expanse of country, mainly desert. It covers a roughly pear-shaped area of about one million square miles, situated between the Red Sea on the west, the Indian Ocean on the south, and the Persian Gulf on the east. On the north are the countries now called Jordan and Iraq.

Judean refugees had begun to settle in Arabia as far back as 586 B.C. when Nebuchadnezzar destroyed the first Temple. Since then, after every upheaval or war in Palestine, and particularly since the Roman destruction of the second Temple in A.D. 70, thousands of Jewish fugitives had found their way south to Arabia.

Here again they began their missionary work among the pagan Arabs. Sometimes whole tribes became Jewish. In the fifth century A.D., the ruler of Yemen, in the south of the Arabian peninsula, was converted to Judaism. Jewish power there continued until the country was conquered in 525 by a combined Christian force of Byzantines and Abyssinians. Some of the oases, especially those in western central Arabia, were entirely Jewish. Jews are credited with having introduced date palm cultivation into Arabia. In the towns they were famous as goldsmiths and in other kinds of skilled crafts, and even as poets and poetesses in Arabic. In the oases they were usually organized on the same tribal lines as the pagan Arabs around them.

But the Jews were not the only monotheistic people in Arabia. There were also small pockets of Christians, even before the Christian conquest of the Yemen. For, in the early centuries of Christianity, where there were Jews there were also almost inevitably Christians. In that period, it was usually Christianized Jews who spread the Gospel of Jesus. But in Arabia Christian missionary work was not as successful as in the Roman West.

Against this background, in A.D. 570, Mohammed was born. He was the son of an Arab caravan merchant of Mecca, then a pagan pilgrim center in western Arabia, about forty miles from the Red Sea coast. Traveling with the desert caravans since early boyhood, as far afield as Palestine and Syria, Mohammed talked with, and learned from, all the people he encountered.

A strange mixture of mystic and practical businessman, at the age of forty he had a vision of his divine mission to convert his fellow Arabs to a belief in the one God. He preached strict Jewish monotheism and

The New Challenge

adopted the Jewish rite of circumcision, as well as a good many of the Jewish dietary laws. He made his followers fast on the Day of Atonement and face the Holy City, Jerusalem, in their prayers. In his writings, which came to be called the *Koran*, he incorporated a large amount of Jewish history and legend. Not surprisingly, he looked on the Arabian Jews as his natural allies and expected them to accept him as the last of their prophets.

Mecca's pagan "elders" were outraged by Mohammed's campaign to destroy the town's innumerable idols, for Meccan prosperity was mainly based on the rich profits of trade with the thousands of pilgrims to the city's many shrines. Mohammed and his followers were threatened and then persecuted. In 622, he barely escaped assassination.

He fled to Yathrib (modern Medina), a twenty-square-mile oasis of villages and farms, about 250 miles north of Mecca. Originally it had been settled entirely by Jews, but by then several pagan Arab tribes were established there, too. These people had become familiar with their Jewish neighbors' ideas about the one and only God of the universe. They therefore found it easy enough to follow Mohammed's teachings, which he usually illustrated with Arabian backgrounds, stories, and poems. Many accepted his new faith, which he called *Islam*, or "submission" to God alone.

But Mohammed was amazed, hurt, and eventually outraged by the persistent rejection of him by the

Yathrib Jewish tribes. Some of their poets even made fun of him. He took his revenge. To begin with, he discarded some of the Jewish customs in his new religion. One day, in the middle of prayer, he suddenly ordered his followers to face Mecca instead of Jerusalem. Then he replaced the Day of Atonement, the twenty-five-hour Jewish fast, by a daylight fast for the whole Arab month of Ramadan. And eventually, as the numbers of his followers continued to increase, he felt strong enough to hit back at the Jews themselves. He attacked one tribe after another, driving them from their homes and fields. To some of them he gave the choice of accepting Mohammed as the Prophet of God or dying by the sword. Many were massacred, and their wives and children made slaves.

Mohammed's power continued to grow, and he went on conquering one place after another. In the ten years between his escape to Yathrib and his death in 632 the whole of Arabia became his.

His successors, the "Caliphs," began where he left off. As Arab tribesmen, fighting and raiding had been the chief occupation of most of Mohammed's followers from the earliest days. They had always been courageous. Mohammed removed their fear of death altogether. He taught them that any Moslem who died fighting for the faith went straight to an everlasting life in a paradise of palm groves, clear streams, fine food, and beautiful women. It was a paradise that no poor, thirsty desert warrior could hope to achieve in any other way.

The New Challenge

The Moslems believed fanatically in their Prophet and his teachings. As long as one idol remained standing anywhere in the world, Mohammed's mission could not be fulfilled. At the same time, there was the prospect of even more immediate rewards in this world. There was loot to be had in each of the rich, decadent lands of Egypt, Mesopotamia, Syria, Persia, and Greece —perhaps even farther west.

With Arabia in their hands already, they now faced a tired, exhausted world. To the north and west lay Byzantium, torn by everlasting rivalry and even bloodshed between its various Christian sects. To the east were the pagan Persians, who lacked even the uniting force of a common religion. Their subject peoples were held down by force alone. These two empires had been bleeding each other white in war for centuries. They were ripe for conquest. Furthermore, when the time came, the long-suffering subject peoples of both empires would very likely help the invaders. Even allowing for all this, the speed with which the Arabs subdued these empires amazes historians to this day.

However, as the victories continued, the Arabs realized that they could not go on slaughtering all the conquered peoples who refused to embrace Islam. Besides, they were finding it impossible to govern the hundreds of thousands who had obediently accepted Islam in the wake of their advance. The victorious Arabs were used to a tribal system, to dealing with small units of people in small isolated communities. They soon found it beyond them to administer the huge, highly sophisticated cities they had conquered. Once the original civil authorities were removed there was chaos.

So the Arabs were compelled to abandon part of their war aim—that of forcing Islam upon the vanquished. Jews and Christians, who believed in one God, were left more or less unharmed. After all, Mohammed himself had respectfully referred to them as the "People of the Book," that is, the Bible. So now only the conquered pagans were given the terrible choice between Islam and death.

The Arabs began to rely on the Jews and the Christians in their occupied territories to run their expanding empire. Jews and Christians were still treated as second-class citizens, forced to pay special taxes, forbidden to carry arms, allowed to ride only donkeys instead of the horses reserved for Moslems, but otherwise they were left in comparative peace.

The Arabs went on to conquer Egypt, Palestine, Syria, Mesopotamia, and Persia. But Constantinople, the capital of Byzantium and its surrounding Christian territory, resisted stiffly. The Arabs bypassed it and continued west along the North African coast. But they had a serious setback in what is now Algeria. At the end of the seventh century they were halted there by a strong force commanded by a Jewish queen and prophetess named Diah Cahena. Possibly a descendant of the priestly Kohanim family, she ruled over a mixed collection of North Africans, Jews, and Christians. For several years her subjects held the invaders

The New Challenge

by "scorched earth" tactics. Whenever the Africans had to retreat, they destroyed towns, villages, crops, and forests, leaving the Arabs without food or fodder. Finally, in a last stand at the beginning of the eighth century, Diah Cahena was killed. The way to the northwest African coast was open to the Arabs.

In 715, less than a hundred years after Mohammed had first proclaimed his new religion, his followers left their African base and crossed the narrow Straits of Gibraltar to invade Spain. From Spain they went over the Pyrenees into France. There, in 732, Charles Martel, grandfather of the future Emperor Charlemagne, defeated them in a great battle at Tours, putting a halt to the Moslem conquest of Europe from the west.

In spite of this, the Arabs might still have crushed Europe with the other arm of their huge pincer. For while one set of Arab forces marched into Europe from the west, several thousand miles away another huge Arab army was trying to force a gateway over the Caucasus Mountains in the east. Here, too, they found their way barred—this time by Tartar converts to Judaism, the Khazars.

Originally a pagan people, the Khazars lived on a large tract of land stretching from the Crimean peninsula on the Black Sea in the southwest and Kiev in the northwest to east of the Caspian Sea and south to the Caucasus Mountains.

Jews had traded there for many centuries. Some had settled permanently, and there is archaeological evidence of Jewish communities in the Crimea as far back as the first century A.D. In about A.D. 700, the Khazar king, Bulan, and many of his court adopted Judaism. This is supposed to have happened after a public debate between Christian, Jewish, and Moslem scholars as to which was the best religion. One of Bulan's successors, with the Hebrew name of Obadiah, built synagogues all over the kingdom and invited Jews from neighboring countries to settle there.

Nevertheless, Khazaria's Christian, Moslem, and pagan minorities had complete religious freedom. The Supreme Court, for example, had two Jewish judges, two Christians, two Moslems, and one pagan. An early Arab historian describes how the Khazar Moslems in the capital had a large "Cathedral Mosque" for their Friday prayers.

For the most part, the Khazars were on good terms with their Christian neighbors in Byzantium, too. Khazar princesses married into the Byzantine Royal Court, even became empresses. The son of one of these became the emperor known as Leo the Khazar.

These people held the Arabs on the Caucasus Mountains. In a hundred years of wars, beginning in the very early days of Islam in 642, victory sometimes went to one side and sometimes to the other. At one time the Arabs were able to overrun a large part of Khazaria. At another, the Khazar victors chased the fleeing Arabs into Mesopotamia itself.

The Islamic advance in the east was stopped at a final battle in 737, only a short time after the Arabs'

The New Challenge

great defeat in the west, at Tours in France. The huge initial impetus of the Arab advance had spent itself.

If either arm of the Arab pincer had succeeded, the history of Europe and of the rest of the world would have been very different. Quite unintentionally, the Jewish Khazars had saved Christian Europe from Islamic conquest. But for the European Jews it was a calamity.

JEWISH GOLDEN AGE UNDER ARABS
· XI ·

UNLIKE THE JEWISH KHAZARS, AND THE JEWISH QUEEN Diah Cahena in North Africa, the Spanish Jews were quite happy to welcome the Arabs when they began their conquest of Spain in 711. In fact, some of them may even have helped the invaders. For to the Spanish Jews, the invincible desert invaders could hardly produce worse horrors than they were already enduring under their Christian rulers. Jews had been in Spain probably even before the first exile to Babylonia. They had found life there comfortable enough until 589. Then the mass of little kingdoms that made up Spain at the time adopted Christianity. And almost at once they began an all-out campaign against Judaism.

Jewish Golden Age Under Arabs

As things turned out, the Moslem rulers treated the Jews better than they could have hoped. The conquest opened a golden age for Spanish Jewry, which, apart from a few brutal interruptions, lasted for more than five hundred years.

In the four years between 711 and 715 the Arabs occupied the whole of Spain, except for a small isolated corner in the north. And they carried their new policy of tolerating Christians and Jews in conquered countries much further now. Both communities were given complete religious freedom and even a great deal of internal independence. The Jews had their own law courts to deal with internal matters. These were not just for civil cases, but for criminal cases also; they could even impose death sentences. In addition, they were completely integrated with their neighbors, Moslem and Christian. There were Jewish ambassadors, scholars, scientists, merchants, landowners, peasants, skilled artisans, livestock dealers, manufacturers, financiers, and even officers and men in the army.

The Arab conquerors were not only filling Spain with beautiful palaces and fountain-filled courts, they also established centers of learning all over the country. The people of Spain—Moslems, Jews, and Christians—were developing not only literature and philosophy, but also the sciences, from mathematics and astronomy to navigation and medicine.

For Arab Spain, at that time, was carrying the torch of civilization in an otherwise dark age. Few people in Europe could read or write except the clergy, who used Latin for written communication. They, too, waited eagerly for every scrap of learning that came out of Spain. A long time later this learning was to help Europe to pull itself out of the Dark Ages.

In this the Jews of Spain played an important part. It was they more than anyone else who brought learning to Christian Europe. Very few Arabs knew Latin; there was no reason for them to bother with the language of uncivilized barbarians. But it was quite different for the Jews. They frequently traveled to all parts of Europe, either on trade missions or to exchange information with other Jewish communities on religious matters. They could hardly do this without at least a working knowledge of Latin, the international language of the Christian world. Many Jews soon became masters of the language and translated important works of literature, philosophy, and science from Arabic or Hebrew into Latin so that these volumes could reach the Christian world.

Among the rich, learned, and powerful Spanish Jews of the time was Hasdai ibn-Shaprut (915-970), a court physician and an ambassador of Abd-al-Rahman III, the Moslem ruler of Spain. Knowing Latin, ibn-Shaprut was able to negotiate with the Christian kings in their own language, from the emperor of the Holy Roman Empire in the West to the emperor of Byzantium at Constantinople in the East.

Samuel ibn-Nagdela (993–1060) in Málaga was

vizier (chief minister) to the king of Granada. For about twenty-five years he more or less ruled the kingdom, even leading its armies in battle. A man of many talents, on the eve of a battle he would sit down to compose elegant poems to commemorate the occasion.

Another important figure was Shlomo ibn-Gabirol (1021-1056), a poet and philosopher. His philosophical work seeped over the mountains into Christian Europe, where it was taken to be Spanish *Christian*, and was used for religious studies. Not until the nineteenth century was it discovered that the author was a Jew.

These are only a few outstanding examples of highly influential Spanish Jews of the period. What is particularly interesting about all of them is that no matter what their daily occupation, or how weighed down with worldly work they were, they always found time for the study of Judaism. They were also in constant communication with Jewish religious authorities in the other centers of Jewish learning. They were particularly close to the Mesopotamian community, although the influence of this culture was by now almost at an end.

Hasdai ibn-Shaprut's Hebrew poems, for instance, are used to this day in the Jewish prayer book. Samuel ibn-Nagdela was a great Talmudist and compiled an excellent dictionary of biblical Hebrew. He also supported poor Jewish scholars not only in Spain but in the Jewish centers of learning elsewhere. To the Jews of Spain he became known as "the prince."

However, at the end of the tenth century, the unified Arab rule of Spain began to break down into small, rival kingdoms, which often intrigued against one another. This gave the semi-independent Christian kingdoms in Spain their first chance to assert themselves. In some cases they even dared to attack some of the weaker Moslem rulers.

Even when the Christians became fully independent, they still practiced the principle of religious toleration that the Arabs had introduced. The Christian kings continued to employ Jews in important positions in their courts and armed services. When Alfonso VI of León and Castile conquered Toledo in 1085, the Spanish Arabs called for help from the Almoravides Moslems of North Africa. The two armies, with many Jews on both sides, were all set for a great battle at Sagrajas. Both Alfonso and the Moslem general agreed that fighting should not start until the three Sabbaths—the Moslem Friday, the Jewish Saturday, and the Christian Sunday—were over.

The Moslems were victorious. But the North African Almoravides were a puritan sect. They were convinced that the reason for the Moslem decline in Spain was their toleration of the "infidel" Christians and Jews. They succeeded in reuniting the Moslem parts of Spain under their own rule, gradually discarding the principle of religious freedom. In 1107 they even tried to force the most influential Jewish community in Spain to accept Islam.

Jewish Golden Age Under Arabs

However, as time passed, so did their fanaticism. Like the early Arab conquerors, the Almoravides came to realize that they could not govern a majority of non-Moslems without religious toleration. Once more, there were Jewish doctors, astronomers, and statesmen with great influence.

Unfortunately this did not last long. The little Christian kingdoms gathered strength and again began to harass the Moslems with raids and small-scale wars. The Spanish Moslems made another appeal to North Africa. In 1146 a violently fanatical North African Moslem army sailed over to Spain. Like that of the original Arab armies, its war cry was "Accept Islam or die!"

Conversion to Islam was easier for Jews than for Christians. The only completely alien dogma they had to accept was that Mohammed was the Prophet of God. A great many Jews therefore decided to conform and become Moslems—at least for the time being.

Many others escaped to more tolerant countries. This time, for a change, it was the Christian kingdoms in Spain that were ready to receive them, although a good many went farther afield than that. By 1172 not a single openly professing Jew was left in the Moslem part of Spain.

One of the families who left Spain altogether was the Maimons. They crossed the Mediterranean to Morocco in North Africa. But their hopes of finding Moroccans more tolerant at home than in Spain were soon disappointed. If anything, religious intolerance in the new country was even more fanatical. Soon the Maimons were forced to pay lip service to Islam and accept it. But they took the first chance that presented itself to move on and finally arrived in Egypt.

There they found a haven of refuge—and even more. Although the Egyptian government was also Moslem, its rulers were tolerant and kind to their Jewish and Christian subjects, who at that time still formed the majority of the population. The Maimons could declare themselves Jews again and become part of the prosperous and influential Jewish community.

One son, Moses, born in Cordova, Spain, in 1135, was thirteen when the family fled to Morocco. In Egypt he was destined to become world famous as Maimonides—the Greek form of the family name. His reputation as a medical doctor was so great that Saladin, the Moslem general who defeated the armies of the Third Crusade, appointed him his personal physician. Maimonides' fame spread so far, in fact, that Saladin's opponent, King Richard the Lion-Heart of England, invited him to become his own doctor. He refused. But Maimonides' medical writings spread so widely that doctors went on studying them as late as the sixteenth century.

His most lasting fame, however, was as a Jewish scholar. He classified the whole of Jewish religious teachings according to their underlying principles. In addition, he came very near to producing a revolution

Jewish Golden Age Under Arabs

in Judaism itself. Judaism had always been more of a "way of life" than a "way of belief." But Maimonides injected a good deal of philosophy—analysis of belief— into it which had not been there previously. He introduced the Thirteen Articles of Faith, which every Jew *must* believe. Until then, belief in one God and His law was enough to make one a Jew. To believe in the coming of a Messiah and the resurrection of the dead had been accepted by Jews for centuries. But until Maimonides' Thirteen Articles they had not been essential dogma.

Also, he moved away from literal interpretation of the Bible. He even explained some biblical prophecies in logical terms. For instance, he maintained that all the biblical commands about Temple sacrifices had simply been part of an attempt to wean the early Jews away from sacrifice to idols.

All these new ideas of Maimonides stirred up a passionate controversy in the Jewish world. It lasted for generations, and almost split Judaism in two. As time went on, Maimonides became accepted by Jewish communities all over the world, and even now his Thirteen Articles of Faith are recited every day by all religious Jews.

So it was that while the Jewish centers of study were drying up in the Moslem countries of North Africa and Spain, Maimonides, a Spanish-born Jew, helped to revive Jewish learning in another Moslem country, Egypt.

Far away in Mesopotamia, also under Arab rule, the last flickering light still glimmered in the Jewish community. Rabbis all over the world still referred their problems to the directors of the Mesopotamian colleges. The Exilarch, the political leader of the Mesopotamian Jews, was treated with great respect by the Moslem rulers. When he went to court, he dressed in the luxurious and costly robes of the noblemen of the time and rode through the streets with an escort of Moslem and Jewish horsemen, with heralds to proclaim his coming. The Caliph, reclining on the royal divan, would rise to welcome him, then wave him to a throne opposite his own. And all the other assembled princes would rise to their feet in respect.

Nevertheless, because of troubled internal conditions, Mesopotamian Jewry was rapidly slipping downhill in its devotion to the study and development of the Law. The final blow came with the Mongol invasion in 1258 under the command of the grandson of Genghis Khan. Baghdad, the capital of the Arab Empire in the east, was sacked and its population massacred. The happy chapter of Mesopotamian Jewish history, which had lasted very nearly two thousand years, from the original exile to Babylonia to the Mongol invasion, came to an end. Jews continued to live there, many of them even making a comfortable living. A few remain there still, but their influence on Judaism and on the Jews of the rest of the world has completely vanished.

There existed yet another important center of Jewish

Jewish Golden Age Under Arabs

learning under Arab rule—Palestine. While Jewish scholars in other places had concentrated on the Talmud and its further interpretations and commentaries, scholars in Tiberias, Palestine, went back to the original, the Bible itself.

Between the eighth and tenth centuries they managed to do a complete survey of the Bible. They also standardized the Hebrew language. They introduced vowels, which made reading Hebrew a much simpler business, for every Hebrew root word is based on three consonants. Until this standardization the vowels that fitted each word could only be understood from the context. Obviously, this could cause great confusion. For instance, if English worked in the same way the three consonants F-N-D could be read as FiND, FouND, FieND, FiNED, ofFeND, FuND, FoND.

Taken as a whole, the period from the seventh century to the twelfth was generally a successful and happy one for the Jews under Islam. It had started badly in Arabia itself and ended badly in Spain and North Africa. Yet in the five hundred years between, the Jews, together with the Arabs, kept the torch of civilization alight in a dark age. With Jewish assistance, Arab culture ruled the world. When the partnership between the two dissolved, Arab civilization started to decline.

DARK AGES IN EUROPE
· XII ·

ON THE WHOLE, UNDER THE ARABS, THE JEWS HAD several centuries of tranquility. They were able to devote themselves to developing their religion and their culture. And they were allowed to be partners in the golden age of Arab civilization.

During the same period the story of the Jews under Christian rule outside Spain went from bad to worse. They had lost their great protector, the Roman Empire. Although the Romans had destroyed Jerusalem and Jewish national independence, it was, ironically enough, the Romans with their famous Law who became the lifeline of the Jews in their exile. Even after the empire became Christianized and deprived the Jews of so many

Dark Ages in Europe

rights, their lives and livelihoods were still protected by Roman Law.

But the Roman Empire in Europe crumbled away into countless little kingdoms, bishoprics, dukedoms, and princedoms, frequently at war among themselves. In the everlasting fighting and raiding, trade hardly existed. Nobody's life was safe for long.

After the collapse of the huge empire there came a new order, the feudal system. This gave the owner of land almost unlimited rights over the people who worked on it. They lived or died at his whim.

But Jews could not own land. The Christian church forbade it. They could not even rent it, because this would involve swearing allegiance to the owner in the name of the Trinity, and this, of course, no Jew could do.

Jews in the cities were not much better off. All skilled workers were bound together in their own guilds, ancestors of today's trade unions. But the guilds were open only to Christians.

The Jews, therefore, were left with very few ways of making a living. One was the practice of medicine. In this they already had a long tradition. The Talmud, of course, gave attention to hygiene and medicine. There was also a long history of Jews as court physicians.

Another avenue open to the Jews was importing and exporting—when there was any chance of doing it in peace. The primitive Christian world consisted of landlords, their semi-slave peasantry, and skilled workers.

There was little demand for trade. But each small country lacked some of the essentials of life, and had a surplus of others. This was where the Jews came in, for they had Jewish connections outside the country they lived in, and these contacts provided a chance to buy and sell goods.

Unfortunately, there was not much they could do with their profits from this business, because they were not allowed to own land. They could, however, lend their cash at interest to the various noblemen, who often needed money badly, either for their little wars or just for extra spending. Christians were forbidden by the church to lend money at interest.

As the Jews had to concentrate in the cities, they "belonged" to the local ruler, whoever he was—king, duke, or bishop. He was their only protector, when he wished to be and when he was strong enough. When he did not wish to provide protection, he was quite free to go as far as he liked. One bishop, for example, who bought a town that had a Jewish community, calmly ordered his estate manager, "Have them burned!" However, this kind of behavior was rare. Usually the ruler protected his Jews just as he protected his land or cattle or peasants.

But rulers were often powerless when the religious passions of their Christian subjects were aroused by fanatics. On the whole such attacks were rare and isolated. This remained true until the end of the eleventh century, when the first of the Crusades began.

Dark Ages in Europe

Nowadays, the word "crusade" suggests a struggle to rescue something good and pure from the menace of evil. But to the Jews of that time the Crusades themselves spelled horror on such a vast scale that even today many Jews shiver at the sound of the word.

The start of the First Crusade had nothing to do with the Jews. Its aim was to rescue the Holy Places of Christianity from the Moslems. Eleventh-century Christian pilgrims to the Holy Land returned to their homes in Europe to stir people with stories of the barbaric way the Moslems had treated them, and of how the Church of the Holy Sepulchre in Jerusalem had been destroyed. It was an age when religion, or rather the outward signs of religion, ruled the ignorant masses of Europe. Feeling against the Moslems therefore began to run feverishly high. Also many younger sons of the aristocracy were only too eager to go out and conquer new land, so that they might become landlords like their older brothers. When in 1095 Pope Urban II called on Christians for a Crusade to rescue the Tomb of Christ and to make the pilgrimage safe, he was answered with the wildest enthusiasm.

In France, a man named Peter the Hermit wandered about among the huge crowds that had assembled for the long trek eastward and preached a new holy mission. While these masses of pilgrims, he screamed, were starting a three-thousand mile journey to save the Tomb of the Savior, "Christ's murderers" were still alive and in their very midst, even in their own cities.

This was enough to start off massacres of one Jewish community after another as the Crusaders marched eastward across northern France and Germany. They made no distinctions. Jewish men, women, and children—they had all killed Christ a thousand years before!

The survivors barely had time to pick up the pieces and try to rebuild their lives when a fresh wave of massacres was sparked off by the Second Crusade, nearly fifty years later.

Soon trouble started even in England, which up to then had been comparatively good to its Jews. At first, the persecution of Jews in England was on a smaller scale than on the continent of Europe. But in 1189, when Richard I (the Lion-Heart) was being crowned at Westminster before leaving on the Third Crusade, the property of London Jews was plundered and some of the Jews were killed by rioters. When Richard left the country, the remaining safety of "his" Jews went with him. The massacres spread to Jewish communities in other English cities. At York, where the bishop had traditionally protected his Jews, many of the local barons who owed money to Jewish financiers saw a chance to get the debt records destroyed. The Jews took refuge in York Castle and defended themselves as best they could. But when they realized it was hopeless, and that the mob would break in at any minute, the rabbi and the heads of the families killed their wives and children and then each other.

Dark Ages in Europe

The first Crusaders to reach Palestine treated the Jews they found there no better. As Godefroy de Bouillon's troops fought their way against the Moslems into Jerusalem, killing everyone in their path, they deliberately sought out the Jews for complete extermination. The steep narrow streets ran with Jewish blood, and any survivors were rounded up into a synagogue, which was then set on fire.

Europe in the Dark Ages was not just fanatically intolerant about religion. It was also unbelievably superstitious. Only a a handful of people could read and write. Life was ruled by unrestrained emotion and fear. Strangers, from another nation or even another village or town, were always suspected and disliked. But one of the most important differences between people then was religion, and of all people with different religions the Jewish neighbors who had "killed Jesus" were the most different.

England was the last country during the period of the Crusades to massacre its Jews. But it was in England that another horror—the "Ritual Murder" libel—started. At Easter, 1144, the body of a boy named William was found in a wood near Norwich. Very soon a rumor spread that "the Jews" had killed him in mockery of the Passion of Jesus, and to celebrate their Passover.

Rumors, even if they were more common, took longer to spread then, without radio, t.v. or telephone. Eventually, merchants and soldiers and wandering priests and courtiers transported this rumor far across Europe. A charge of the same kind in France in 1171 meant the burning of almost a whole Jewish community. It happened again in Paris in 1180, and later in many other places.

However much eyewitness evidence had been produced by the normal method of the time—torture—the rulers very rarely believed these stories. But the masses did believe and were frequently encouraged in their belief by the almost equally ignorant local priests. Shrines were often built to these child victims, and sometimes miracles were reported from them. William of Norwich was even made a saint.

After some of the Jews at Valreas, France, had been tortured and then burned, Pope Innocent VI issued a "bull," an official papal letter, to all the French and German bishops stating that the accusations were untrue. The popes had made life very difficult indeed for the Jews in the lands they directly ruled, but they did not wish them to be destroyed—Jews, alive but in misery, were the best proof of the curse that had been laid on them. In fact, Jews in the papal states were in general far better off than those in the rest of the Christian world. There was every possible kind of discrimination against them, but their lives at least were safe.

For centuries Christians had been taught to hate the Jews because they had killed the Saviour. The next step was to hate the Jews as personal enemies who were for-

Dark Ages in Europe

ever plotting the destruction of their Christian neighbors. If a Christian fell ill after meeting a Jew, this was obviously due to Jewish magic. If the crops failed, it was because the Jews had cast a spell on them with the help of their ally, the devil.

The ground was therefore well prepared for blaming the Jews for the terrible Black Death of 1348. This appalling epidemic—probably bubonic plague—killed about one quarter of the population of Europe. In some countries the percentage was even higher. Everywhere the Jews, who followed the hygienic laws of their religion, seemed to suffer far less than other people. That was proof, if proof had been needed at all, that the Jews were responsible. By magic or by poisoning the wells, or both, the "Christ killers" had set this horror loose to destroy the Christians, the servants of Jesus. As a result, all over Europe Jews were burned alive. Scores of thousands of Jews were added to the victims that Europe's lack of elementary hygiene had already claimed.

EXILE FROM EXILE
· XIII ·

PEOPLE WHO LIVE ON THE SLOPES OF A VOLCANO KNOW quite well that they are liable to die sudden and agonizing deaths when the mountain erupts and lashes out streams of deadly lava and suffocating gases. Yet no sooner has the volcano gone back to sleep again, deep in the bowels of the earth, than the return of the survivors begins.

Back they trek to their burned-out homes, their devastated gardens and orchards and fields, deep in the ashes. Patiently they clean and clear and sow and build. They pick up the pieces of their past and tie them to the hopes of a future.

It was exactly this that the Jews did in their exile.

Exile From Exile

They were always picking up pieces, eternally hopeful of a brighter future. After every massacre—by fire, by sword, by torture, by burial alive—the survivors trudged back to start building again on the ruins of the past.

A few, supreme optimists, might even manage to persuade themselves that lightning does not strike twice in the same place. A catastrophe that had recently wiped out their relatives and friends could not possibly happen again. After all, they told themselves, their Christian neighbors were human beings. Surely they must regret the horrors they had committed in a fit of madness.

Other survivors were less optimistic. Some were downright pessimists. They looked back into their history and saw that each madness bred more madness—that it was catching. All the same, they too went back to their ruined homes and the tortured ghosts of their loved ones. Where else could they go? Where *was* safety?

In one way or another, the survivors would start afresh, eating, sleeping, bringing new children into the world, praying in their synagogues for deliverance by the Messiah, who would take them back to a free and independent Palestine. They studied Judaism. They wrote sad Hebrew poetry about the tragedies that had befallen them. Some of these became part of the Jewish prayer book.

But even this did not last long. Only too soon any new hope was swept away, along with the people who nourished it. For there came a devastation unlike any the Jews had experienced since they were driven from Judea centuries earlier. This time it was an exile from exile itself.

England gave the lead. There had been a number of expulsions of Jews in other parts of Europe before, but they had affected only small communities, the property of some local lord or of a weak king who had little influence over his barons.

But Edward I of England was a strong king who had his dukes and barons well under control. He insisted that all the Jews throughout the entire kingdom were his own property. He himself fixed the rate of interest to be charged by the Jewish moneylenders, raising it higher and higher, and taking a larger and larger percentage of it for himself. Whenever he needed extra money he simply told the heads of the Jewish community that he must have such and such a sum by such and such a date. Somehow or other the Jews would have to raise that money among themselves. It was made very clear to them what would happen if they did not.

By 1290 the English Jews had been drained of most of their property. Even Edward realized that there was nothing more he could get out of them. So he ordered the expulsion of every Jew from the kingdom of England and at the same time seized any of their remaining property that he could lay his hands on. This terrible decree was made on the ninth of Av, the anniversary of the destruction of the Temple in Jerusalem.

Exile From Exile

The Jews crossed the English Channel to France. But they did not find much safety there. As the French king's power over his lesser lords increased, and the French Jews were made poorer and poorer by the king's demands for larger and larger sums, catastrophe struck there too. In 1306 the king of France ordered the expulsion of all Jews from his country, first, of course, confiscating their property.

For the second time within sixteen years the Jewish exiles from England had to move on. Along with the French Jews, who had helped them to find new homes, they wandered off in search of yet another resting place.

In the meantime, the profession of money lending had been taken over by Christians. They had found a way around the church prohibition, but their terms for repayment and interest were so savage that a popular French song of the period ran:

> *For the Jews were debonair*
> *Greatly more in this affair*
> *Than now the Christians are.*

In 1315, the new French king, Louis X, invited the Jews to return. But seven years later Charles IV expelled them again. In 1359 they were asked to come back, and in 1394, accused of persuading baptized Jews to return to their original faith, they were banished yet again.

Germany, on the other hand, had no central government. There was, therefore, no general expulsion of Jews there. But massacres of Jews by mobs of frenzied Christians went on, in one place or another, throughout the various German states, almost without a break. Usually, only an individual community was attacked, so that the survivors were able to find shelter with Jews in neighboring towns, but quite often onslaughts were made on the Jews of several towns at the same time. Then there was no escape. In 1298, 146 flourishing Jewish communities in Germany were wiped out.

However, as if by a miracle, a refuge for thousands of surviving Jews did suddenly appear. This was Poland.

That country had been more or less laid waste in the middle of the thirteenth century by Asian invasions. Eventually, these invaders were driven off, but Poland was almost devastated in the process. It had hardly any cities, industry, or commerce left. So, Casimir the Great, the king of Poland, welcomed Jewish enterprise, and in 1354 gave the Jewish arrivals a generous charter, offering protection and even a great degree of self-rule.

Poland had only two classes left—a top layer of nobility, the owners of vast estates, and a bottom layer of their miserable serfs. The new Jewish immigrants built up market towns, administered the estates of the nobles, collected the excise and other taxes, and sometimes even leased estates to run themselves. They managed salt mines and timber mills and imported and exported goods.

They brought with them their own special language,

Exile From Exile

which was called *Jüdisch*, or Yiddish. This was—and is still—the German of medieval times written in Hebrew characters and fortified with a good many Hebrew words.

As time went on this language was used in Jewish communities everywhere, except in countries where the Spanish exiles predominated. In each country it gathered up a few local words, so that the Yiddish of the United States, for instance, became distinct from the Yiddish of Russia. The exchange was two-way. Many Yiddish words have now become part of colloquial English and American; *nosh* (snack), *schnorrer* (beggar), and *meshugga* (crazy) are examples.

In the intervals between one exile and another the Jews in Western Europe who survived the massacres built up for themselves a spiritual fortress. This was their unquestioning faith in their religion and the unity of the entire Jewish community, which was always ready to help any member in trouble. As a reminder of Jerusalem—as if one was needed—an unpainted patch was left on every Jewish house as a symbol of mourning.

This spiritual strength was fortified by the home—by the development of family love and affection. Wife-beating, for instance, must have been very rare among the Jews. A medieval rabbi called it "a Gentile practice."

But the actual physical home might have been made of straw for all the protection it provided. By expulsion after expulsion the Jew was driven from it. One of these expulsions became the most notorious, and the worst, because it affected a very large number, and because they had been the richest, strongest, and most influential of all Jewish communities in Europe. This was the banishment of the Jews from Spain in 1492.

After the Christian rulers of the various Spanish kingdoms gained the upper hand over the Moslems, the Jews there were still treated well. The Christian kings were acutely jealous of one another and everlastingly trying to grab one another's territories. So they were quite ready to make use of Jewish skills and intelligence in every sphere, as diplomats, doctors, scientists, financiers, administrators, and soldiers. For years they had politely ignored the constant reminders about the church's anti-Jewish laws that came from pope after pope. Alfonso VI, king of León and Castile from 1065 to 1109, had a Jew as his personal doctor. He often consulted this man on state matters and even allowed him to countersign official documents. On one occasion when Alfonso's Jewish ambassador was ill-treated by the Moslem ruler of Seville, the affair led to war. At this time in other parts of Europe Jews were being slaughtered in the thousands by the Crusaders.

Little by little the popes' reminders ate into the Spanish Jews' security. The Christian kings in Spain felt compelled to make laws forbidding Jews to hold positions of trust. But they took very little if any notice of them in actual practice.

Exile From Exile

Unfortunately for the Jews, the situation was quite different among the ordinary Spanish people, who were very much under the influence of their local priests. In 1108, after the Castilian army had been defeated in a battle, a rumor spread that its left flank, which was manned by Jews, had been the first to give way and retreat. At once, in Toledo, the capital of Castile, a mob rioted and attacked the Jewish community.

As Moslem rule in Spain grew steadily weaker, this kind of attack became more and more frequent. Constantly, the priests helped to raise the religious fever of their flocks by preaching against the Jews. And on Ash Wednesday 1391 an anti-Jewish sermon sparked off a violent attack. As the religious fanaticism spread from one Spanish kingdom to another, more than seventy thousand Jews perished.

Thousands, however, saved their lives by accepting baptism. Many became genuine and enthusiastic Christians—some even to the point of leading anti-Jewish campaigns.

For many others, however, the conversion was for appearances only. They attended mass and confession, had their children christened, but secretly went on keeping as many of the Jewish laws as they dared. They, and their descendants for several hundred years, snatched at any chance to get to some place abroad where they could live openly as Jews again.

These thousands of Jewish converts were officially known as "New Christians," although the man-in-the-street preferred the term "Marrano," which means "swine." Many of these New Christians rose socially, married into the nobility, and even reached the top ranks of the church.

But this escape through baptism turned out to be only a mirage. Soon a new danger arose, this time from the leadership of the church itself, the dreaded Inquisition.

This institution, the Holy Office of Questioning, was set up in Spain in 1480 with the express purpose of rooting out all Christian heretics and sinners. Six months later, six New Christians, accused and found guilty of secretly practicing Judaism, were publicly, and with full religious and state ceremony, burned alive. From then on, these public burnings (*autos-da-fé* or "acts of the faith") became as much a part of normal Spanish life as bullfights are today.

The Inquisition published lists of clues by which friends, neighbors, and relations could detect any backsliding New Christian. One clue was putting on clean clothes on Friday afternoon before the beginning of the Jewish Sabbath. Torture usually produced the necessary confession. Sometimes "old" Christians— those who were attracted to Judaism by the heroism of the Jews who died for their faith—or persons otherwise branded as heretics, suffered the same fate as the New Christians.

Altogether the Spanish Inquisition and the later Portuguese Inquisition condemned more than 375,000 people, most of whom were New Christians. Nearly forty thousand of them died in public *autos-da-fé*. They came from all classes and professions. In Portugal, in only eight years, fourteen nuns and six friars were burned to death. The torture of victims, followed by death at the stake in the name of the religion of love, went on in Spain and Portugal and in their vast colonies overseas until the end of the eighteenth century. Even now, in remote parts of Portugal, there are supposed to be a few New Christians left, who still quietly keep up some Jewish traditions.

The New Christians probably often envied their openly Jewish cousins, or at least those of them who had managed to escape baptism as well as death from mob violence. For they, at least, were not "heretics," and could not be touched by the Inquisition. Again, once the volcanic eruption passed, the surviving Jews drew another breath and began afresh. Once more, the Spanish kings made full use of their talents, appointing them to all kinds of important offices.

But as Moslem rule in Spain gradually disappeared, the power of the Spanish church increased. Spanish kings were forced to make even greater concessions to their bishops, at the expense of the well-being of their kingdoms.

The final climax began with Isabella, queen of Castile. In 1469 Isabella married Ferdinand, heir to the throne of Aragon, uniting the two most powerful kingdoms of Spain. It is ironical that this marriage, which was arranged only after long negotiations conducted by an important Jewish financier and a New Christian, was fatal for the Spanish Jews.

The blow came in 1492. This was after the Moslems had lost Granada, their last stronghold in Spain, bringing to an end their seven-hundred-year rule. Now the leaders of the Spanish church could demand— and get —a Spain exclusively Christian, without a Jew in it. That same year Columbus discovered America, which would become the refuge of the oppressed and the persecuted, including millions of Jewish refugees. Yet to Jews this date remains one of the major dates of tragedy in their calendar. For in March 1492 Ferdinand and Isabella, rulers of most of Spain, ordered all Spanish Jews expelled. At least 150,000 men, women, and children trekked to the frontiers or the ports, with bands playing to keep up their spirits. Thousands of others avoided exile only by accepting Christianity.

It is this expulsion that mention of the year 1492 conjures up in the minds of most Jews today—this, and the oath of the departing Jews that never again would any Jew set foot on Spanish soil. Generations kept this oath faithfully. Today Spain has only a tiny community of Jews, who are comparatively recent settlers. Some of these, ironically enough, are refugees from the terror of Nazi Germany.

Yet the love of the Spanish Jews for the country in which their ancestors had settled about two thousand years before remained very deep. The descendants of

Exile From Exile

the exiles, as well as those of the New Christians who escaped in later centuries and re-adopted Judaism, still speak a language called "Ladino." This is fourteenth-century Castilian Spanish, the language probably spoken by Columbus and his sailors. They still cling to their Spanish and Portuguese names—García, Da Costa, Henriques, Mendes. Some of them in the Middle East and North Africa still put on traditional Spanish dress, all frills and mantillas, for festival days.

The fanatical religious leaders of fifteenth-century Spain had their way at last. Within a short time there was not a single professing Jew left in Spain or in the territories then under its rule, such as Sardinia and Sicily.

Economically, politically, and militarily Spain seemed to be riding the crest of a great wave. Everywhere it was expanding its power—through conquests, and still more by the discovery of America and the ruthless exploitation of its vast riches. And, of course, the Spanish Crown had also confiscated almost all the wealth of the Jews it had sent into exile.

Actually, however, 1492 was the beginning of Spain's long downfall. All the gold of the Americas, all the plunder from the Jews was of no use if it was not made to work. By destroying its Jewish community, Spain demolished the main foundation of its trade, finance, and general economy. It is one of the historical examples of a nation suffering for its crimes.

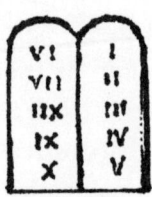

MIRAGES AND HAVENS
·XIV·

WHAT HAPPENED TO THE 150,000 REFUGEES FROM Spain? Where did they go?

Famine and plague killed many. Others were robbed, murdered, or sold into slavery by the ship captains they had paid to carry them to freedom. Even those who escaped these particular fates were not always that much luckier. The starving fugitives, as they came off the ships at Genoa, Italy, were met by friars carrying a cross in one hand and a loaf of bread in the other, offering food for the price of baptism.

About a hundred thousand refugees crossed the Spanish border into Portugal, where craftsmen with special skills or any person who could pay with gold for

Mirages and Havens

the privilege were allowed to settle. All the others were charged a large fee for a permit to stay for eight months; those who were financially able often paid for those who had no gold. At the end of that time, the Portuguese king declared that he would sell as slaves all those who had not left.

When the king died, his successor, Manuel, gave the Jews their liberty. But this relief did not last long. The king's fiancée, a daughter of Ferdinand and Isabella, refused to set foot in Portugal until it was cleansed of all unbelievers. So in 1496 the king issued an order for all Jews to leave Portugal within ten months.

He was not at all eager to have this edict carried out, for he had already seen that the talents of the new immigrants could be extremely useful for the development of his country. He thereupon issued a new command which, to the devoted Jews, was far more horrifying than expulsion. This was nothing less than the forced baptism of all Jews, without the alternative of leaving the country. He began by ordering the baptism of all Jewish children between the ages of four and fourteen. When the soldiers came to drag the children away, many parents killed their own children and then committed suicide.

Soon after, Jewish adults were driven to the churches in droves, holy water was sprinkled on them, and they were pronounced Christians. After this, they were frequently herded into church for mass, although otherwise they remained Jews more or less openly. When in

1531 the Inquisition began to function in Portugal as well as in Spain, life became unbearable for these unhappy Portuguese Jews. Once the water of baptism had been sprinkled on them, they were totally under the authority of the Inquisition, with its torture and burning of heretics.

They adjusted to the new conditions, hiding their Jewish practices. They prospered in every field of Portuguese life. They intermarried with the aristocracy, and in time there were hardly any high-ranking Portuguese who had no New Christian family connections. There is a story about a king of Portugal who wished to order all descendants of New Christians to wear a particular kind of hat, so that they could be recognized. His minister came to him and laid three of the special hats on the table before him.

"What on earth are those for?" demanded the king.

The minister bowed.

"One is for myself," he said, "one is for your Majesty, and the third is for the Chief Inquisitor."

But many of these Spanish and Portuguese Marrano Jews remained faithful to their old religion and avoided any marriage with outsiders. The devotion of so many Jews to their religion, without regard to the appalling cost, may best be illustrated by the following story. A Jewish exile from Spain succeeded in finding a ship to take him and his family to Africa. He was the only member of the family, however, to reach a safe destination. His wife was raped and then taken away, and his

Mirages and Havens

children were carried off to be sold as slaves. He stretched out his hands toward heaven and cried: "Lord of the Universe, thou hast done much to make me abandon my faith. But know that, notwithstanding those who dwell on high, I am a Jew and a Jew I will remain!"

However, a large number of the Spanish exiles did in the end find a haven. This was Turkey, the new Moslem Empire centered in Constantinople, which fell to the Turks in 1453. The sultan of Turkey received the Jewish exiles with kindness. He realized how valuable these new arrivals—craftsmen, scientists, doctors, statesmen, experts in trade and finance—could be to his empire.

"How can this Ferdinand be called 'wise,' " he demanded, "when he depopulates his own kingdom to enrich mine?"

As it happened, many of the exiles rose to high positions in Turkey. The Jews did actually help the sultan to develop his empire. They vitalized trade and industry. The first books printed in Turkey were in Hebrew. Jews manufactured gunpowder and other armaments for Turkish forces. They made Salonika (now in Greece) the greatest trading city in the eastern Mediterranean. In fact, Jews were the majority of the population there, working as traders and fishermen, manufacturers and stevedores. Soon after they arrived, Jews became personal physicians to the sultans and ministers and ambassadors too.

The most famous of the exiles to succeed spectacularly in Turkey was a later arrival, Joseph Nasi, whose name in his native Portugal had been Joao Miguez. His parents were among the Jews who left Spain for Portugal rather than accept baptism. But in 1497, they had been forcibly converted, and his father was then appointed personal physician to the king. Joseph's aunt, Beatrice de Luna, was married to the wealthy head of the banking and jewelry firm of Mendes. When he died, she moved to Antwerp (then a Spanish possession) to run the firm's important branch there. She took Joseph with her.

Beatrice's daughter, Reyna, was very beautiful, and the queen regent of the Netherlands wanted her to marry one of the court favorites. Beatrice said firmly that she would rather see her daughter dead.

After this, she thought it wise to leave the country and find a safer spot for herself and the family. After many adventures they eventually arrived in Constantinople. Here, at last, they were free to throw off their Christian disguise and become Jews openly again. Beatrice became Grazia Nasi, and Joao Miguez, now Joseph Nasi, married his beautiful cousin Reyna.

Joseph rose to a high position at the sultan's court and was appointed Duke of Naxos, one of the Greek islands. At one time he was the most influential person in the huge Turkish Empire. He was able to revenge himself on Spain by encouraging the revolt of the Netherlands against Spanish rule.

Joseph Nasi also tried to reestablish a Jewish Palestine

in the second half of the sixteenth century, by human means—not waiting for the miracle of the hoped-for Messiah. He persuaded the sultan to grant him the ruined city of Tiberias, on the Lake of Galilee, with a stretch of land around it. Some of the refugees from Spain and Portugal had made their way to Palestine, after overcoming the fantastic difficulties of travel at that period. They helped to swell the small existing Jewish communities there.

These new settlers, however, were chiefly pious Jews, who went to Palestine to be close to God. They were anxious to forget both their prosperous beginnings and the torments of their downfall. One of these, a rabbi, planned to reestablish the ancient Sanhedrin, as a supreme authority on Judaism. But his attempt failed because of the opposition led by another rabbi, who had been forcibly baptized in Portugal in his youth.

These Jews devoted themselves to Jewish studies and prayers and little else. Most of them lived on the charity collected from Jewish communities outside Palestine, for Jews everywhere were eager to support these servants of God in the Holy Land. It made them feel that they, too, had a share in their devotion.

Joseph Nasi realized that these small religious communities were no basis for the rebuilding of a Jewish state in Palestine. First, he rebuilt Tiberias and fortified it. Then he began to introduce a textile industry there. He planted mulberry trees to provide food for silkworms. He imported merino wool for weaving. He invited skilled Jewish workers from every country to come and settle there. He even sent out his own ships to the papal states to transport Jews to Palestine.

But the time for this was not yet ripe. Jews who had known only torture, burning, expulsion, re-settlement, and exile once again had abandoned any trust in their own human efforts. They believed fervently that the only hope lay in the supernatural arrival of the Messiah, who would lead them back to Palestine and deliverance.

This kind of mysticism led various rabbis, particularly in Palestine, to develop another branch of Judaic studies, the Cabala. This concentrated on the hidden meanings of God's commands, the origins of the universe, the nature of God Himself. It was a collective Jewish escapism into a spiritual world where enemies could not penetrate.

Given this mysticism, and the general Jewish belief that Jewish sufferings at the time were so appalling that this must be the dark hour heralding the dawn, the field was wide open for false Messiahs. Quite a number of them began to appear.

One was Diogo Pires, a young Marrano, who was a promising government official in Portugal. He escaped from Portugal, and openly followed Judaism under his ancestral name of Solomon Molcho. After devout study of the Cabala, he became convinced that he himself was the Messiah. He warned the pope of a coming flood disaster in Rome, which, in fact, occurred on

Mirages and Havens

October 8, 1530. This impressed the pope so much that he offered the heretic Molcho the hospitality of his palace. When the Inquisition demanded that Molcho should be released to them for burning, the pope is supposed to have handed over a criminal who looked like Molcho instead.

Molcho's belief in his mission was so strong that eventually he left his refuge with the pope and went to the emperor of the Holy Roman Empire to proclaim himself Messiah. But this time his mission ended in disaster. He was handed over to the Inquisition and burned alive in 1532 at the age of thirty-two.

Molcho was only one in a long line of false Jewish Messiahs, who continued to crop up well into the eighteenth century. Some sincerely believed themselves to be the messengers of God. Others were out and out frauds. Both types found followers among the suffering Jewish masses.

SUNRISE IN THE WEST
·XV·

THE COMPULSORY BAPTISM OF JEWS IN PORTUGAL turned out to be no more successful in the long run than the mass conversion of Spanish Jews under threat of death. For generation after generation, great numbers of New Christians secretly kept faith with Judaism. Many others managed to make their way to the Spanish and Portuguese territories in the New World of the Americas or to refuges in Europe, Africa, and Asia.

But as long as the Marranos remained under Spanish or Portuguese rule, they were the target of the all-powerful Inquisition. The slightest suspicion that they were not faithful Christians would bring down torture, burning, and confiscation of their property by the church.

Sunrise in the West

However, many were lucky enough to escape to *Christian* countries where the Inquisition was less powerful or had no power at all. These countries were influenced by the tolerant spirit of the Renaissance or had broken away from Roman Catholicism to form the Protestant churches.

Marranos settled in various Italian kingdoms, in the south of France, and in some of the German states. They still kept up the pretense of being Christians. But the authorities in these countries made very little attempt, if any, to find out whether these New Christians were really genuine servants of Christ. Other Marranos were more fortunate still. They had gone to Holland, which after a long and bloody struggle had succeeded in breaking free both from bondage to Spain and from Roman Catholicism. There, in time, the Marranos were able to declare themselves openly as Jews. They established the first official Jewish community there as early as 1606. The Jewish community in Amsterdam eventually became so prosperous and influential that people sometimes called it the "New Jerusalem."

Jewish enterprise helped Holland to become the leading trading nation in the world and to build up a vast empire. Now the New Christians were leading merchants, bankers, and diplomats again, but as Jews and not as Marranos.

In the intellectual field, too, they distinguished themselves. Baruch (Benedict) d'Espinoza, usually called Spinoza, born in 1632, was a great philosopher and had a tremendous influence on the development of Western thought. But the Jewish religion, mainly concentrating on ethics and morals, had never really encouraged philosophy for philosophy's sake. Eventually, the Jewish community of Amsterdam came to believe that some of Spinoza's teachings were contradicting a part of Judaism, and he was excommunicated.

But Spinoza himself never became converted to Christianity. Once when asked whether Judaism was better than Christianity, he replied: "All religions that lead one to a good life are good. You need not look any further."

Another Amsterdam Jew of the period, remarkable for very different reasons, was a rabbi who had been one of Spinoza's first teachers. This was Menasseh ben Israel, whose Marrano parents had fled from Portugal to Holland when he was only a year old. He was brilliant even in his extreme youth and was ordained as a rabbi at the age of eighteen. He was married to a great-granddaughter of Don Isaac Abrabanel. Abrabanel had been a personal friend of King Ferdinand and Queen Isabella, but in 1492 he had led the Jewish exiles out of Spain.

Apart from his office as rabbi, Menasseh ben Israel wrote books on Judaism. His main aim was to correct mistakes and misunderstanding about the Jewish religion that existed among Christians at the time, even the most learned ones. His books brought him many friends. One of them was Queen Christina of Sweden.

Sunrise in the West

Another was the artist Rembrandt, who painted a portrait of Menasseh that is now famous. In history, however, Menasseh ben Israel was important for something completely different—his negotiations with Oliver Cromwell, Protector of England after the Revolution and the execution of Charles I in 1649. Menasseh wanted Cromwell to legalize the resettlement of Jews in England.

At the time many Christians in Western Europe believed firmly that the Second Coming of Christ must be preceded by the dispersal of the Jews into every corner of the earth. (Another belief of that time was that the American Indians were the Ten "Lost" Jewish tribes.)

Menasseh ben Israel, too, believed in this "dispersal" theory, although, of course, his expected Messiah was not Jesus. He, therefore, saw the return of Jews to England as a step in the right direction. Cromwell, on his side, realized quite well what the Jews had done for the prosperity of Holland and thought that England could do with some Jewish enterprise, too.

There were already a few hundred Jews in England at the time. Some of them had been there even in the second half of the sixteenth century, in the days of Queen Elizabeth I. But they were there completely unofficially—illegally to all intents and purposes.

All Cromwell's efforts to persuade his countrymen to allow a new influx of Jews on an open, legal basis failed. In 1656 he summoned a conference on the subject. At once rumors spread that Jews were trying to buy St. Paul's Cathedral in the City of London for a half a million pounds. However, the real problem lay not with such fantastic ideas among the people, but within the sober and serious conference itself. The lawyers could find no legal objection, but the City merchants were nervous of Jewish competition. And the clergy raised the strongest objections of all. "They raged like fanatics," according to a report of the time.

In the end, no resolution was adopted at all. However, Cromwell assured Menasseh ben Israel that it would be perfectly all right for Jews to come and settle in England. Provided that they observed their religion quietly and did nothing to draw attention to themselves, they would be protected from possible attack. But there could be no official recognition.

Menasseh went back to Holland heartbroken, and died a year later. When Charles II came to the English throne after the Restoration, in 1660, he wrote in the margin of an official document that things should go on as before. Jews could settle in England, but without any special charter.

For the Jews of Continental Europe, the dawn was at last breaking. In enlightened Western Europe there was now little taste for massacres of Jews, not even in the little German states. Dark and backward Spain and Portugal now had no Jews at all. They had to content themselves with festive public burnings of suspect New Christians or sometimes "old" ones. In Protestant

Sunrise in the West

countries Marrano refugees could declare themselves Jews again without fear of the consequences.

Superstition had declined enough to make it impossible to accuse the Jews of calling up Satan to spread disease among the Christians. Accusations that Jews had to procure Christian blood for the Passover Festival had become extremely rare, although there have been occasional attempts to dig up that libel even in our own day.

But it was only dawn breaking—a faint light on the horizon, not really enough to see the way safely. The lives of Jews were secure in most West European countries. They could practice their religion—in some places completely freely, in others under various restrictions.

One thing they still lacked—equality. Unlike their Christian neighbors, they existed on sufferance, not by right. For their protection and safety, they had to obtain special charters. There was always some condition or other that Jews had to fulfill and Christians did not. Jews were not citizens, they were simply tolerated foreigners.

Then, at last, the sun, which had been such a long time rising, began to warm up. It shone brightly first in the West, in France, the country that had started the mass extermination of Jews at the beginning of the Crusades. The slogan of the French Revolution of 1789 was "Liberty, Equality, Fraternity." Even Jews could not be fenced out of this promised paradise.

Soon, under Napoleon Bonaparte, the victorious

French armies were marching through Europe. Into one country after another they carried the banner—"Liberty, Equality, Fraternity." And they smashed down the walls of the ghettos in which the church had deliberately segregated the Jews from the Christians. Venice had originated the name *ghetto*. In carrying out strictly, in 1516, church orders for the segregation of Jews, it had herded them into a special quarter called Getto Nuovo (New Foundry). On July 10, 1797, the people of Venice, in a festive mood, tore down the ghetto gates and made a bonfire of them. In Rome itself, deliverance of the Jews came a few months later, in February 1798.

However, with the fall of Napoleon in 1815, a reaction set in in many parts of Europe. Holland and France were the only countries that continued to give their Jews full equality. In the papal states, which included Rome, Jews were forbidden once more to live anywhere except within the ghetto walls. Nonetheless, even there the Jews were no longer forced as they had been before to wear a special badge so that Christians could recognize them at a glance.

Some of the German states revived a number of restrictions on the Jews. There were even places where mobs attacked Jews and beat them up. They would do this shouting the old slogan "HEP! HEP!" which went back to the days of the Crusade massacres. H.E.P. are the initials for "Jerusalem is lost" in Latin.

Some talented young Jews gave up all hope of suc-

Sunrise in the West

cess if they remained Jews, and had themselves baptized. One of these was Heinrich Heine (1797–1856), who was to become one of Germany's greatest poets.

The nineteenth century was a succession of ups and downs for the Jews of Central Europe and Italy. Various countries underwent waves of revolution in the middle of the century. And when these were crushed, the Jews lost many of their hard-won rights. In Rome, for instance, the church even brought back the medieval rule that Jews must be assembled forcibly at intervals to listen to sermons by Christian priests. Jewish children were sometimes kidnapped, baptized, and never allowed to see their parents again.

But the spirit of liberalism, which had begun to spread through Europe at the end of the eighteenth century and the beginning of the nineteenth, eventually conquered one center of reaction after another. In 1870 the pope lost his states, including Rome itself, which became the capital of a united Italy. At this, the oldest Jewish center in Europe was, at last, able to breathe the fresh air of freedom, and hope that this time it would be forever.

In England, one restriction on the Jews lingered on to a later date: Jews still could not hold any office of state. At last, however, in 1858 a Bill was passed giving each House of Parliament power to provide by resolution for the admission of Jews. Baron Lionel de Rothschild was the first Jew to be made a Member of the House of Commons after this change. Later, in the early 1870's, another Jew, Sir George Jessel, was appointed Solicitor-General, one of the highest offices of English justice.

The great nineteenth-century English Prime Minister, Benjamin Disraeli (1804–1881) is often referred to as a Jew. He was, in fact, baptized as a child; yet, throughout his life he remained very proud of his Jewish origin.

The last of the West European states to break down its barriers against Jews was Switzerland. As late as the middle of the nineteenth century Jews were not allowed even to enter some Swiss cantons. However, the United States, England, and France brought pressure to bear, by refusing to do business with Switzerland until the laws were changed. And in 1874, Switzerland gave Jews full equality.

This new liberal attitude of west Europeans toward the Jews gave them the chance to take part in the Industrial Revolution of the nineteenth century. They grasped the opportunity eagerly, with all their pent-up energy and ability. For the past thousand years or so Christianity had made the Jews a town people, driving them out of the villages and agriculture into trade and finance. In the fantastic economic expansion of Western Europe in the nineteenth century, this turned out to be a blessing, for the boom in industry chiefly affected the towns and cities. And the Jews were townspeople.

Western Europe became the world's workshop. It manufactured goods and machinery and sent them off

Sunrise in the West

to all the corners of the earth. Jewish traders, with their age-long experience, their worldwide family connections, and their knowledge of languages, were tailor-made to play a leading part in the development of international trade.

The same was true of finance. Capital on a huge scale was needed for the development of factories, mines, railroads, and shipping. The Jewish financiers of the past had been limited to local moneylending. Now they were quick to grasp the opportunities, which the new conditions presented, to operate on an international scale. They not only provided capital, they created it, by the new banking system that enabled people to pay out money in their hometown and have it collected abroad by someone else. Before that, a load of gold could only be transferred by a special messenger.

A large number of Jewish financiers played a vital part in banking. But one name has become a household word everywhere—that of Rothschild. Its founder, Meyer Amschel (1743–1812), was financial agent to the ruler of one of the small German states. His five sons settled in London, Frankfurt-am-Main, Germany; Paris, France; Vienna, Austria; and Naples, Italy. They took their name from the Red Shield that had marked the family house in the medieval Frankfurt ghetto.

All the Rothschild brothers engaged in large-scale finance, working as a team. In 1875 the British government gained control over the Suez Canal, which would become the fastest route to their empire in India, with money advanced by the London branch of Rothschild.

It was not just in trade and finance that Jews distinguished themselves during the nineteenth century. Some of them also became outstanding industrialists, inventors, scientists, doctors, lawyers, politicians, musicians, writers, and publishers. A few of the more famous Jewish names of the time are Paul Reuter (1816–1899), who developed the transmission of news from one place to another; Adolph Ochs (1858–1935), founder of *The New York Times*; Albert Ballin (1857–1918), who established the Hamburg-America Steamship Line.

Ludwig Mond (1839–1900), an immigrant to England from Germany, laid the foundations of the chemical industry in his new country. His son, Lord Melchett (1868–1930), built this up into the vast Imperial Chemical Industries (I.C.I.). Adolphe Crémieux (1796–1880), was French Minister of Justice in 1848 and 1870–1871. He abolished slavery in the French colonies, as well as capital punishment for political crimes. Sir Julius Vogel (1835–1899) was Prime Minister of New Zealand in 1873.

Naturally, there were many famous Jews in medicine. Paul Ehrlich (1854–1915), the great bacteriologist, is known chiefly for his discovery of the "Magic Bullet," a cure for syphilis. The research of Waldemar Haffkine (1860–1930), another bacteriologist, saved millions of lives from bubonic plague. Sigmund Freud (1856–1939) was the founder of psychoanalysis.

Jews also showed a tremendous interest in science.

Sunrise in the West

The most outstanding of the world's scientists was a Jew of our own century, Albert Einstein (1879–1955). His new theories were responsible for the development of atomic energy.

Jewish inventors include David Schwarz (1845–1897), who built the first dirigible airship; Moritz Jacobi (1801–1874), who in 1831 built the first motorboat; Siegfried Marcus (1831–1898), one of the first inventors of the motor-car. Gabriel Lippmann (1845–1921, of Paris discovered the process of color photography.

The list could go on and on, of course, and famous Jewish musicians, painters, and actors and theatrical, film, and television producers have not even been mentioned.

West European Jews, of course, made the most of their new freedom. Their energy, enterprise, passion for learning, resilience, adjustability, and organizational powers came out in a flood. The dam that had held them back for so many centuries had suddenly burst wide open.

Naturally, the Jews themselves benefited a good deal by this. But the real profit went to the countries that had now begun to treat the Jews as human beings. In the nineteenth century the Jews did for those countries what they had done for Holland in the seventeenth and for Spain from the eighth to the fifteenth century.

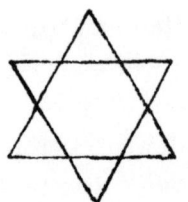

SUNSET IN THE EAST
·XVI·

AT THE VERY SAME TIME THAT LIFE WAS BECOMING easier in general for the Jews of Western Europe, in Eastern Europe the situation was exactly the opposite.

Jewish refugees from Western Europe had been flocking into Poland to escape massacres since the fourteenth century. Polish king after Polish king followed the example of Casimir the Great, who in 1354 had granted the Jews a charter that gave them protection and a certain amount of self-rule. The Jews had done well for themselves and even better for the Polish kings and for the country as a whole. They had built up a healthy economy in a country that before their coming had lain waste as a result of invasions and wars.

Sunset in the East

The kings themselves were delighted with the progress and happy with the Jews. But the superstitious, downtrodden, ignorant, and still semi-slave masses felt very differently. To begin with, they were jealous of Jewish success. Envy turned into hatred as Jews became managers of the great estates of the noblemen and had to carry out the unpleasant orders of the lords to the serfs.

. Sometimes Jews even leased estates and became masters themselves, with all the friction with workers that this situation so often brings. Even as importers and exporters the Jews were blamed whenever the price of foreign goods went up or the price of Polish exports went down.

In this situation any fanatic could have fanned the simmering economic envy into a blazing religious hatred of the "Christ killers." But the kings were strong enough to protect the Jews and faithfully kept to the terms of their charters. For about four hundred years the Polish Jews were the safest and most prosperous of all the Jewish communities in Europe.

But in the middle of the seventeenth century, just as light was beginning to dawn for West European Jews, in Poland darkness descended. In 1648, the Cossacks of the Ukraine, mainly wild shepherd tribesmen, rebelled against their Polish landlords. The rebellion was basically for economic reasons, but it had a religious motive too. The Cossacks had been converted to Christianity about six centuries earlier. Like the Russians farther north, they had adopted the Greek Orthodox version. They therefore hated the Roman Catholicism that the Poles tried to force on them.

But the Cossacks hated the Jews—the "Christ killers" —even more than they hated the Catholics. To this horde of illiterate and savage tribesmen, the Jews were the real enemy, even economically. For, as stewards, tax collectors, mill and mine managers, the Jews were the stick with which the Polish landlords beat them. Led by their chief, Chmielnicki, the Cossacks galloped in on their fast shaggy ponies, burning and slaughtering, with the Jews as their first target.

The rebellion and the raids went on and on. Then, in 1654, the czar of Russia came in on the Cossacks' side and invaded Poland. City after city in Lithuania and what is now called White Russia fell to the Russians and the Cossacks. Mad with religious fanaticism, they exterminated or expelled the Jews of each place as they occupied it. In the ten years between 1648 and 1658 a hundred thousand Jews perished in this way. Thousands of penniless survivors managed to fly westward, to be sustained by the charity of the more fortunate Jews there. Others found refuge in the Turkish Empire.

Yet the cup of misery was still not full for the many survivors who stayed on either because of misplaced hope for the future or because they were too weak, physically, mentally, or financially, to run for their lives. Local, small-scale attacks and petty persecutions

Sunset in the East

became almost a matter of routine. In 1767, another rebellion in the Ukraine against the Poles sparked off further massacres of Jews, on the scale of those 120 years earlier.

Polish Jewry was finally broken. Its prosperity never came back, even when conditions settled down. More and more thousands of Polish Jews escaped to the West. But most of those who survived the periodic attacks remained—to be persecuted and forced deeper into poverty. For Poland was torn by wars and rebellions, was conquered by Russia, broke free, was conquered again. In the end, in 1796, it was partitioned, with Austria, Germany, and Russia each getting a share.

Russia got the largest slice. From then on there was even less hope for the Jews. Of all the Christian sects, the Russian Provoslav Church, a branch of the Greek Orthodox, stood out as the most fanatically intolerant toward Jews. Even before Russia got hold of the main part of Poland, Catherine II, in 1762, had granted permission to travel in her country to all nationals of all religions—except Jews. When nobles from western Russia protested that they needed the Jews to manage their estates and businesses, she replied: "I do not wish for profit from the enemies of Christ."

The official position of the Jews in that part of Poland annexed by Russia worsened tragically. For hundreds of years they had lived under a government that had protected them and given them a chance to make a living. Now the new government deliberately tried to get rid of them, or, if this failed, at least to degrade them. They were forbidden to move anywhere east of western Poland, which came to be known as the "Pale of Jewish Settlement."

Even in the places where they were allowed to live the Jews suffered all kinds of restrictions and persecutions. The orders came from the central government, and petty officials or local police made their own harsher interpretations of these orders.

Czar Nicholas I, who came to the throne in 1825, wished to reintroduce the medieval practice of forced baptism. But in the nineteenth century, even Russia, the most backward part of Europe, felt unable to revive the cry "baptism or death" of the eleventh to fifteenth centuries. Nicholas therefore decided to modify the ancient practice—bring it up to date, as it were. He ordered all Jewish boys to be taken from their parents at the age of twelve to be "educated" for army service.

Instruction during these six "educational" years was divided between army sergeants and Christian army chaplains. At eighteen the boys were to join the non-Jewish conscripts, who were drafted at that age for the general twenty-five years of compulsory military service.

But Nicholas' method of Christianizing the Jews was no more successful than were the earlier attempts in Spain and Portugal. No doubt the six "educational years" broke down a good many of the captured children and turned them into Christians. But many man-

Sunset in the East

aged to endure that indignity and the twenty-five years military service, with its curses on Jews and Judaism, far from their Jewish homes and backgrounds. A century later, Golda Meir, granddaughter of one of these tortured boys, was to become Prime Minister of the reborn Israel.

Easier years for the Russian Jews came under Alexander II, who was czar from 1855 to 1881. He was considerably influenced by Western liberal ideas and abolished the conscription of Jewish children into the army. He reduced the period of military service for everybody from twenty-five years to six.

Alexander also allowed selected Jews to settle in Russia proper, east of the "Pale." In the "Pale" itself, Jews were given a few new rights and could even be elected to the local councils, which Alexander had established. Nevertheless, he left the three million Russian Jews as miserable economically as his ancestors had made them.

In 1881 Alexander was assassinated. In order to divert the attention of the people, who were beginning to organize themselves for revolution, the government spread a rumor that Jews had done the killing. At once there were attacks on Jews wherever they lived. In some places the army openly took part. Then the Russian word *pogrom*, meaning "devastation," became internationally known as an officially inspired massacre. From time to time, these pogroms recurred, even into the early twentieth century. One high Russian churchman told a Jewish delegation that his policy for solving the Jewish problem was to kill a third of the Russian Jews, drive out another third, and convert the rest to Christianity.

In Western Europe, Christian countries, which a few centuries before had been treating Jews in much the same way, were now, in their new, tolerant civilization, horrified at what was happening in Russia. Their ambassadors at St. Petersburg (now Leningrad) delivered official protests from their governments. But the new czar, Alexander III, like the pharaoh in ancient Egypt, simply ordered new restrictions on the Jews.

A large-scale exodus of Jews from Russia began. At the end of the nineteenth century and the beginning of the twentieth hundreds of thousands fled. A majority found their haven in the United States. Smaller groups settled in other countries, chiefly in Britain. To the end of their lives, these refugees could not forget the horror of their youth. Year after year, the approach of Easter, with its reminders of the crucifixion of Christ, would make them shudder, remembering how in the "Old Country" their homes had had to be darkened, their doors bolted and windows shuttered, against attacks of mobs out for revenge on the "Christ killers."

SETBACK IN WESTERN EUROPE
·XVII·

THE ENLIGHTENED LIBERALISM OF THE EIGHTEENTH century in Western Europe developed fully in the nineteenth. And it was this, of course, that delivered the Jews from darkness to light.

In Western Europe life was no longer colored, as it had been in medieval times, by the expectation of the "End of the World" and a doom-laden "Day of Judgment." The more blatantly stupid and harmful superstitions, too, had been cast off. By the eighteenth century many people could read and write. They had studied the Old Testament as well as the New. They knew that in the Old Testament drinking or eating or cooking with blood was forbidden to Jews, and so were witchcraft and any "dealings with the devil." Jews could not possibly want blood for their Passover nor were they likely to make pacts with the devil.

Religion, or rather that mockery of religion which had been the uniting force in Europe in the Middle Ages, was losing its power. But something else had to take its place.

This turned out to be nationalism, comparatively new to Europe. Before Christianity, the various tribes and little kingdoms had been ruled by the Roman Empire. Later on, the empire's role had been taken over by the pope, although local kings and barons did govern their own lands and people in day-to-day affairs. But their subjects had a *personal* loyalty to the lord or king, not a national one. A French-speaking overlord, for instance, could own land both in France and in Germany. He could call on both his French and German subjects to fight for him against other Frenchmen and Germans.

In country after country strong kings gradually emerged. Each was able to unite a whole set of local chiefs into one kingdom under his personal authority. And once a king had achieved supremacy in his kingdom, his next ambition was often to shake off his chain of bondage to the pope as ultimate ruler. The feeling of kinship and brotherhood people had had for their fellow villagers gradually grew to embrace all the subjects of the same king. Little by little, loyalty to king became loyalty to king *and country*.

The first country in Europe to achieve a strong

Setback in Western Europe

centralized, united nationhood was England. Henry VIII not only had complete mastery over his kingdom, but went so far as to cut his religious ties with Rome, to make his country independent of the pope, spiritually as well as materially.

Nationalism, in fact, enlarged a collection of small early tribes into one huge tribe. These modern tribesmen recognized each other by a common language, customs, traditions, background, and, above all, by religion. And in all of them the Jewish neighbor stood out as someone apart.

His history was strange. It went back thousands of years, through all the countless countries where his ancestors had lived, to Palestine. His customs and traditions, even his special foods, were all utterly alien. He prayed in a synagogue, not in a church, and in Hebrew, for the coming of a Messiah who was not Jesus, and who would take him back to Palestine. Jews by this time were free to do any kind of work they wanted to. But after work they were apt to retire to their homes and have very little to do with non-Jews.

Most reasonable Christians, especially in the Protestant countries, were now quite ready to forget the old legend of the Jews as "Christ killers" and forever accursed. They were happy to allow the Jews to live among them in safety.

But many could not bring themselves to accept their Jewish neighbors as members of their own nation. They went on regarding them as foreigners. The law had granted Jews full citizenship, with equal rights and duties, but it could not force the ordinary Gentile to think of them as full members of the nation.

These people had not thought out their criticism of the Jews properly. For centuries, Christian society had driven Jews from the land. The church had confined them to ghettos to keep them apart from the Christians. Even before the ghetto became compulsory, Jews liked to live near one another for protection. There was slightly more safety in numbers, and the walls that kept the Jews in after sunset sometimes helped to keep Gentile mobs out.

Even though things seemed to be safe at last, the nightmare of past massacres was so deeply ingrained into the Jewish make-up that Jews still went on searching for the warmth and assurance that went with having other Jews near them. And, of course, it was convenient for them to be near their synagogue, their butcher, and their grocer with the favorite Jewish foods.

The result was that in nineteenth-century Western Europe Jews found two faces turned to them. There was the official one, the liberal-minded government that, for the first time since the Roman Empire, granted them full citizenship and the same rights as their Christian neighbors. And there were the faces of their Christian neighbors, many of whom refused to recognize Jews as equals. Even if a Jew left the synagogue, the ghetto, the butcher, and made up his mind to live like a Gentile, he very often found the door slammed in his face.

Setback in Western Europe

This attitude was not just a nonacceptance of Jews as equal citizens. It is difficult to belong to a group of people of the same kind without coming to believe that group superior to others. With the growth of nationalism had come a belief in national superiority. The people of every nation were absolutely certain that their own standards of morals were superior to those of any other nation. They also had better brains, were kinder, had a keener sense of humor, and were better mannered. When one was not actually at war with neighboring nationals, one could at least curse them or laugh at them.

The world is familiar with the Jewish claim to be the "Chosen People." This is because it was stated in the Old Testament, which had penetrated to every corner of the globe. In fact, almost every nation has laid claim to be the "Chosen."

"Lesser breeds without the Law," wrote the English poet Rudyard Kipling of foreigners—and then, of his own country,

> *Wider still and wider*
> *Shall thy bounds be set.*
> *God who made thee mighty*
> *Make thee mightier yet!*

"*Deutschland über alles!*" sang the Germans. And other lands had other variations.

In daily life very few of these despised foreigners

were visible for people to laugh at or curse. The sense of superiority had to be satisfied by reading horror stories or jokes about foreigners. The villain in stories of the time was almost invariably a foreigner.

However, each country did have a handy supply of Jews—double foreigners, because they were not even Christian. People bought things from them, people sold things to them. They rubbed shoulders with Gentiles on the sidewalks, they sat next to them in trains and carriages. They were always around to be cursed at or laughed at, if not actually to their faces, then back home or with friends in clubs or at work. Their presence went a long way toward satisfying the Gentiles' sense of superiority.

In addition, Jews were everywhere a tiny minority, a weak people, unable to defend themselves against either curses or jokes. There really are very few of them about. Today the total number of Jews in the world is around twelve million, living among 3.5 billion people, or about one in every three hundred. The largest Jewish community lives in the United States, and out of a total population of two hundred million there are five or six million Jews—fewer than six Jews to every two hundred Gentiles.

Thus, with the rise of nationalism, it was quite safe to attack the Jews—in speeches, in papers, and in books—because there was very little chance of being hit back. Alphonse Toussenel, a French socialist, identified the Jews with his pet hatred—the development of capital-

Setback in Western Europe

ism and the cities at the expense of agricultural life. His book, the first to attack the Jews in this way, appeared in 1845 in France, the very country that, under Napoleon, had done so much for Jewish liberty. Apart from this, until quite recently, the development of this new-style anti-Semitism was almost exclusive to the extreme reactionaries.

About ten years later another Frenchman, Count Joseph Arthur de Gobineau, wrote another anti-Semitic book. Waging war against progress, he clung to his title "Count" in a Republican France, which had long before done away with the nobility. He despised the middle and lower classes, which had taken away the power of the upper classes. In his book, this man argued that by nature some human races were masters, some slaves, and some destructive. The master races, he said, were the "Aryans," of whom the French were the leading branch, with their nobility as the supermen among supermen. The "Semites," on the other hand, were natural world-destroyers, and of the Semites the Jews were the most dangerous.

At about this time, too, it appeared that the old-fashioned *religious* anti-Judaism still lived. In 1869, a French Catholic writer published a book that spelled out all the old accusations against Judaism and Jews, with some new inventions for good measure.

In 1871 the French were defeated in the Franco-Prussian War. In 1886 another book was published, blaming the Jews for this.

The real explosion of anti-Semitism came in 1894. Then Alfred Dreyfus, a Jew serving as a captain on the Intelligence staff of the French Army, was accused of having sold secrets to the Germans. To prove this, a colonel produced a document supposed to have been written by Dreyfus. Influential church dignitaries and reactionary royalists combined to start a strong anti-Jewish campaign, in the Parliament, in the press, and on the streets. Shouting his innocence, Dreyfus was sentenced by court-martial, in January 1895, to life imprisonment on Devil's Island, a French penal settlement.

Later a Colonel Picquart, also on the French Intelligence staff, found that Dreyfus' handwriting had been forged by another officer. True liberal France began to stir, to save the soul of the country. The outcry against the sentence on Dreyfus, led by Emile Zola, the famous writer, grew fiercer and fiercer. France was divided into camps—pro- and anti-Dreyfus.

Before long Picquart unearthed more forgeries in the army documents. For this he suffered persecution and eventually imprisonment, but he stood his ground. Eventually Colonel Henri, the officer responsible for the forgeries, committed suicide. The real traitor, the man who had sold secret documents to the Germans, turned out to be yet another officer, a Major Esterhazy.

Dreyfus the Jew was free again and back at work. Other Jews felt reassured for the future, as the reactionary forces scuttled off in disgrace. Even the Catholic

Setback in Western Europe

church in France, which had had a hidden, and often not so hidden, connection with the dark forces that had tried to make Dreyfus the eternal Jewish scapegoat, paid dearly. It lost almost all the state power that had been left to it after the Revolution.

In every part of the world civilized people heaved a sigh of relief. For in the liberal period at the end of the nineteenth century, the Dreyfus case was not merely a French scandal. It shook fair-minded persons everywhere. The world had still not experienced the mass slaughter of millions of people in the two world wars of the twentieth century. Even in their worst nightmares people could not have visualized a Hitler and the "final solution." For a short while, they believed that the sanctity of the life and the freedom of every single individual anywhere was unquestionable.

NEW TRENDS AMONG THE JEWS
·XVIII·

THE JEWISH PASSION FOR EDUCATION WENT BACK TO the very early days. King Hezekiah, in the eighth century B.C., was said to have hung a sword with a slogan inscribed on it on the gate of the Temple in Jerusalem. It declared that anyone who did not learn to read and write as good as condemned himself to death.

The passion for learning became even stronger as time went on. In the fourth century A.D. Rabbi Simon ben Yohai once remarked: "If you see cities uprooted, you can be sure that it came about because they did not pay their teachers big enough salaries."

For nearly two thousand years the way of life of the

New Trends Among the Jews

Jews and the study of the Talmud had held them together. Unlike the earth and stone of their homeland, these things were transportable. The Jews could take them with them wherever they wandered or were driven. The bonds had been tested, under Moslem rule and under Christian rule, in poverty and in riches, in massacres and in security. As the flames of Europe's fires devoured their last breath, Jews would still cry, "Hear, O Israel, God is our Lord, God is One!"

They threw themselves on the Talmud, on its interpretations, on its commentaries—learning, dissecting, arguing. Rules about sacrifices in the nonexistent Jerusalem Temple became as important to them as the rules that governed daily life—their marriages, their food, their hygiene. They began to think that intellect was the most important thing in life. Even people who could barely understand what was being discussed would flock after work to the Talmudic discussions in the synagogues. They listened, they admired, but the scholars took no notice of them.

Side by side with this, later rabbis kept on adding ritual after ritual, ceremony after ceremony to the Judaic principles of social justice. Ritual began to be as important as fundamentals. Sometimes it even seemed more important. There is a small, very strict sect of Jews today who would never dream of celebrating a Sabbath or a festival service in the synagogue without putting on a fur-trimmed hat. This very expensive headgear has an entirely non-Jewish origin. It is simply an imitation of the hats worn by Polish noblemen in the late Middle Ages.

Another thing new to the Jewish religion was the compilation of Jewish law by Rabbi Joseph Caro (1488–1575). When he was a child his family was exiled from Spain. They settled in Turkey, where Joseph made a name for himself as a scholar and mystic. Later he moved to Safed, Palestine, the headquarters of the Cabalists.

But it was as a Talmudist that fame came to Caro. In 1565 he published a vast work called *The Prepared Table*. This set out in plain and simple language all the rules and customs by which Jews are supposed to live. Until then they had been hidden away under countless arguments and discussions and scattered through scores of volumes of the Talmud and its commentaries. Only the very learned could find their way about these easily. Now Caro made it all clear and available to any Jew who could read Hebrew.

Caro's *The Prepared Table* was an immediate success with Jewish communities everywhere. Again and again it was reprinted, as the accepted last word on Judaism. It came at a time of great need for, in one place after another, the church was burning the Talmud itself. And under the terrible conditions of the period Jewish scholarship itself had declined.

The *Prepared Table* was a welcome gift. It regulated the life of a Jew from the moment he woke up to the moment he went to sleep. Eating, drinking, washing, business, family, speech, synagogue, festivals—all had to be "by the book." Some of the rules were inessential points that happened to appeal to Caro personally. But such was the fame of the book that all became equally important.

These developments tended to bottle up Judaism into intellectualism, ritual, and a codified unalterable book of conduct. And they were bound in the end to produce opposition. One of the qualities that in the past had enabled Judaism to survive was its adaptability, its constant adjustment to a changing and developing world.

HASSIDISM

The first rebellion was against intellectualism—the everlasting study of the Talmud. It began in Poland with a simple lime-digger, Israel ben Eliezer (1700–1760), who was later known as Baal Shem-Tov ("the master of the Good Name"). He traveled all over Poland, preaching that devotion to God was more important than scholarship and that any ignorant laborer could come as near to God by serving Him as any great Talmudist could by all his learning.

Israel ben Eliezer's rebellion was also against the gloom that, not surprisingly, overlay the whole of Judaism at that time—mourning for the past glory, agony for the present, fear for the future. He taught the poor, simple Jews of unhappy Poland that serving God with joy and jollity was the highest possible achievement. God did not, he said, want man to serve him by self-denial or self-deprivation. It was happiness and delight, said the master of the Good Name, that could make man one with God. The few who could achieve this state were nearer to God than the rest, and they could even put in a good word for less successful worshipers.

For the Jewish masses in Poland this was an attractive idea. Making any kind of a livelihood was becoming more and more difficult and took up most of their time. There was very little time left for study, and so the ordinary working Jews had become used to feeling inferior to the others because of their ignorance. Now came a man who brought them dignity and self-respect. Furthermore, he was against the constant fasting and general sadness of Jewish ritual at the time, which made their harsh lives seem even harsher.

Soon a new sect was born. They called themselves *Hassidim*—"the pious ones." (Pronounce the initial *H* like the *J* in the Spanish Juan or the *ch* in the Scots *loch*.) Israel ben Eliezer himself was called the *zadik*—"the righteous one", the closest to God of all of them. His prayers for anyone were therefore the most likely to be answered.

The new movement spread quickly all over Eastern Europe, and after Israel ben Eliezer's death other *zadikim* sprang up in several places. Their followers came to them with their troubles and their prayers. Some turned over a share in their businesses to the *zadik*, hoping that this would increase prosperity. Soon it became accepted among the *Hassidim* that the fantastic heavenly powers of the *zadik* were hereditary.

New Trends Among the Jews

On the death of a *zadik* his son almost automatically took his place.

The new "revivalist" sect horrified the Jewish "Establishment." Not only did the *Hassidim* abandon the study of the Talmud. They mixed up their prayers with feasts—and what was more, they drank strong spirits at these feasts and sometimes sang and danced themselves into ecstasies.

The "Vilna Gaon," Elijah (1720–1797), the greatest Talmudist of the time, excommunicated followers of Hassidism. For a while it looked as if Judaism would be split in two. But as time went on the *Hassidim* ceased to object to the Talmud. Some of the *zadikim* were even great scholars themselves.

The Establishment side also gradually relented. Outright condemnation mellowed into poking fun at Hassidism. The following story, obviously fiction, laughs at the faith of ignorant people in the miraculous powers of the *zadikim*.

Two *Hassidim* were arguing fiercely as to which of their two different *zadikim* was better at miracles.

"My *zadik*," said one, "once found himself in his carriage late on a Friday afternoon in the middle of a thick forest. He did not want to desecrate the Sabbath by traveling. But he also did not want to insult it by fasting gloomily in the middle of nowhere. So he lifted his eyes to heaven in prayer. And at once the horses leaped into the air and flew him home with time to spare to put on his Sabbath clothes."

"That's nothing," said the other. "In exactly similar

circumstances, *my zadik* waved his right arm to the right and his left to the left. And you know what happened? There was Sabbath on the left of the carriage. There was Sabbath on the right. But on the road the carriage took, it was not Sabbath at all."

The extraordinary power that the *zadikim* had over their hundreds of thousands of followers, and the unlimited faith the worshipers had in them, probably saved many lives—and more people's sanity. There is a story that illustrates both the deep psychological insight of many of the *zadikim* as well as the unquestioning faith of their followers.

A poverty-stricken Jew, living in a mud hut in a Polish village, pleads with his *zadik*.

"My wife has just died. I have four small children. There is no one to look after them. Business is at a standstill, and there's no food in the house. Rabbi, tell me what to do."

The *zadik* pulls at his long white beard and delivers his advice.

"My son, Moshe down the street has a goat that he wants to sell cheaply. I'll advance you the money. You go get it. At least there'll be milk for the children."

"But *zadik*, there's hardly room for us to move as it is—we've only the one room. Where can I put the goat?"

"There will be," says the *zadik*. "You'll see."

A few days later the man comes back.

"*Zadik!* That goat—it messes the floor, it kicks the

children, it's broken pretty nearly every stick of furniture we've got. And you just can't imagine the stink!"

Again the *zadik* strokes his beard.

"I have the right answer," he says at last. "Go into town and sell the goat in the market. It'll bring in a little money until things get better."

A week later the man returns.

"*Zadik*, you've no idea the wonders you've done for me. The house is clean. There's no stink. And there seems so much more room in the hut, now I've got ride of that goat. Thank you from the bottom of my heart!"

Hassidism laid great stress on the idea of an intermediary between man and God. This seems strange indeed in a religion where each community chooses and elects its rabbi. He is there chiefly as a teacher, not at all as somebody to plead with God for his flock, because before God they are all equal. Whatever its source, Hassidism gave meaning to the lives of hundreds of thousands in many generations of Jews who could not find it in the Talmud. One of the greatest Jewish philosophers of our own century, Martin Buber, fell under the spell of Hassidism.

ASSIMILATION

There was another rebellion within the Jewish people during the eighteenth century, this time in Western

Europe and not focused on the Talmud or the ritual alone. It was directed against Judaism itself—laws, ritual, nationhood, anything Jewish.

For some Jews had had enough of the sword, fire, and exile, all for the sake of a religion that, in the new age of rationalism, failed to attract them. Their dearest wish was to take on the color of their surroundings, to be lost in the great jungle outside. They wanted to be Germans, Frenchmen, Englishmen. Intermarriage between Jews and Christians became common. There is supposed to be hardly one aristocratic family in England—or before Communism in Hungary—without a Jewish ancestor in it somewhere.

The church, the Inquisition, the Russian czars, and the fanatical Moslem rulers had not succeeded in making the Jews abandon Judaism, but the early days of freedom for Jews in religiously tolerant Europe did begin a process of weaning them from their people and their religion. The movement gathered strength as freedom increased. "Assimilationist" Jews cut every Jewish connection, hid anything that might identify them as Jews—names, dress, language, associations. Many went even further and deliberately embraced Christianity. About two hundred thousand Jews are supposed to have had themselves baptized during the nineteenth century alone.

Oddly enough, this assimilation into the world outside had begun with a man who was a conscientious Jew, whose great aim had been to revive Jewish learning,

New Trends Among the Jews

and who had himself been a keen Talmudist. Moses Mendelssohn (1729–1786) was a manager for a Jewish manufacturer in Berlin when he won first prize in an open competition for a philosophical essay in German. He won, incidentally, over the great German philosopher Immanuel Kant. Mendelssohn soon became a "protected" Jew; that is, he was exempted from all the restrictions applied to ordinary Jews. The doors of German society were thrown open to him, and the Jewish communities throughout the German states were very proud.

Mendelssohn wanted to revitalize Jewish learning, to bring it out of the stuffy ghetto and weld it to the modern intellectual development in the world outside. He and his disciples began to publish a literary magazine for poetry, essays, and drama—all in a modernized Hebrew.

But many of Mendelssohn's followers thought that his main aim was to move away from Judaism. Mendelssohn, they thought, was simply compromising—making a beginning. The result was that while Mendelssohn himself remained a strictly observant Jew to the end of his life, after his death hundreds of his followers became Christians. Among them were his own children; his grandson Felix, the composer, wrote some of his greatest music for the Christian church.

Conversion of Jews to Christianity increased as the nineteenth century advanced. But at least these new converts hardly ever turned against Jews or Judaism, as so many medieval converts had tragically done. The outstanding exception was Karl Marx (1818–1883), author of *Das Kapital* and virtual founder of Communism, who was baptized as a baby. His writing against Judaism still influences many of his followers today.

REFORM

Yet another movement away from tradition, Reform Judaism, began in the nineteenth century. Moses Mendelssohn had not wished to change the religious side of Judaism. He just wanted to adjust Jewish culture to that of modern Western Europe.

The later Reformists, however, changed the religious and ritualistic sides of Judaism in their desire to bring them more in line with modern non-Jewish thought and practice. They aimed at getting away from the endless laws and rituals that centuries of ghetto life had wound around them. Their goal was a return to the essentials of Judaism found in the writing of the prophets.

Reform Judaism was born in Germany, where its first special synagogue was opened in 1818. By 1840 England, too, had a Reform congregation. German-Jewish immigrants to the United States introduced Reform even earlier, in 1824, and by the middle of the nineteenth century it was a powerful movement in America.

New Trends Among the Jews

The early Reform movement was a kind of split personality in Judaism. On one side, it brought the Jewish religion, ritual, and synagogue worship as close to Protestant Christianity as it could without actually accepting Christ. It discarded the idea that Jews were a separate people. It removed from the prayer book all reference to the Jerusalem Temple or the return to Palestine. Reformist Jews proclaimed themselves Germans or Americans or Englishmen in everything except religion.

But, on the other side, Reform aimed at stopping assimilation with the Gentile community by attracting all those Jews who no longer wanted ghetto Judaism. It provided an alternative, a middle course. It meant that to escape from the ghetto it was no longer necessary to get baptized or to settle down in a kind of limbo, neither Jew nor Christian.

TRENDS (continued): ZIONISM
·XIX·

THE FOURTH AND MOST RECENT OF MODERN JEWISH trends was political Zionism. It was named for Zion hill in Jerusalem, where the ancient Jewish kings had their palaces.

Political Zionism did not concern itself with the religious side of Judaism. Its focus was on the Jews as a separate people with a right to develop their own full, free nationhood. It was the opposite pole of assimilation and early Reform.

In a purely religious form Zionism was as old as the Jewish dispersal throughout the world. It was part of Jewish Messianism. Throughout the "Diaspora" (the "scattering"), as the post-Roman settlement of the

Trends (Continued): Zionism

Jews outside Palestine came to be called, Jews prayed every day for a return to Palestine. The climax of the Passover ceremony is the hopeful cry "Next year in Jerusalem!"

This deeply rooted faith that God would not desert them forever, and would eventually send the Messiah, helped to keep the faintly glowing embers of Jewish life alive in the darkest times. At the same time it also made the Jews a happy hunting ground for false Messiahs.

The most recent of the more important false Messiahs was Shabbetai Zevi, born in Smyrna, Turkey, in 1626, who declared himself to be the Messiah. in 1648. He was attended and assisted by his "Prophet," Nathan of Gaza, Palestine, and by his wife, Sarah. Forcibly baptized after her parents' death in a massacre, she had reverted to Judaism after escaping from Poland.

In a very short time Shabbetai had a tremendous following among the suffering Jews. Synagogues introduced a new prayer for "our Lord, king, and master, the holy and righteous Shabbetai Zevi, anointed by the God of Israel." Jewish businesses everywhere came almost to a standstill, because most Jews were getting ready for Shabbetai to lead them to Palestine. Jewish businessmen in Holland were packing their bags; in Hamburg, Germany, there was dancing in the synagogue, in Spain and Portugal Marranos made frantic efforts to smuggle themselves out, so that they could march to Palestine openly as Jews.

The excitement about Shabbetai spread beyond the Jews to the Christians. In England, Samuel Pepys wrote in his now-famous diary that there was a Jew in London prepared to bet £100 to £10 that "a certain man from Smyrna would be recognized as King of the World" within two years. Some Christian sects believed firmly that the year 1666 would see the end of the world. It was a tragedy for most of the excited Jews when the story of the new "Messiah" ended in farce. The Turkish sultan gave Shabbetai the choice of death or conversion to Islam, and he promptly accepted Islam.

But for some of the most enthusiastic followers even this was not too much. Some people insisted that it could not have been the real Shabbetai who became a Moslem, but only a phantom. Others explained ingeniously that their deliverer must experience every possible existence before coming out in his true role as Messiah. These people became Moslems themselves, after Shabbetai died in 1676, forming a separate sect in Turkey.

Although the Jewish belief in a Messiah always had an element of the supernatural, it had remained basically earthy and material. True, there was going to be a miracle, but it would be performed by a man of flesh and blood, although he would be inspired and anointed by God. After the shock of Shabbetai Zevi's conversion, the idea of a Messiah moved into a purely miraculous sphere. The anointed was to descend from

Trends (Continued): Zionism

heaven, bringing with him a Temple built "from fire."

In spite of their longing to return to Palestine, the Jews did not believe that they could attempt it by themselves. The Messiah, whether of flesh and blood or heavenly, would have to help them. Of course, some people decided to anticipate the Messiah's coming by settling in Palestine to await him there in prayer and study. There were also a few small and isolated communities of Jews whose ancestors had never left the country at all, somehow surviving the Romans, the Persians, the Arabs, the Crusaders, the Turks, and so on. One of these communities existed until recent years, in a tiny Galilean village, which was part-Moslem and part-Jewish.

The long series of wars and conquests had left Palestine more or less devastated, near-desert. Most of the trees had been cut down for fuel, the ancient hill terraces had collapsed, and the rains had washed the fertile soil down to the plains and the sea. It had become a land of rocky, thorn-covered hills, marshy malarial valleys, and sand dunes. The tiny Arab population was desperately poor and weakened, for the most part by malaria. They had no will or energy, or even the means or knowledge, to improve the land they worked. Their goats skipped and climbed about everywhere, eating up everything green, even gnawing the slim trunks of saplings. And any tree that survived their attacks was eventually cut down by the villagers to be used as charcoal for cooking and heating.

As for the small Palestinian Jewish communities, they were busy communing with God and had no time or thought for improving the soil. There would be no need for earthly food in the days of the Messiah. The only attempt to persuade the Jews to use their own hands to restore a natural, thriving Jewish community had been that of Joseph Nasi in Tiberias in the sixteenth century. But that had failed, and no one tried again until the nineteenth century.

By then there were many Jews, particularly in Russia, who, although they no longer cared very much for the rules of the Jewish religion, still rejected both assimilation and baptism. The civilization of nineteenth-century Russia was extremely primitive, with none of the attractions of that of Western Europe. Nor did the Russian Jews feel drawn to the "religion of love," which had expressed itself in persecution.

To these Jews the idea of nationalism, which by then had conquered Europe, seemed attractive. They clung to their Jewishness as members of a Jewish nation. At the end of the century, when thousands of Jews fled from the pogroms in Russia to the United States, Britain, and other countries, small groups made their way to Palestine.

These people did not go there to pray and await the Messiah. They believed in doing something about Palestine themselves—giving the Messiah a helping hand, as it were. They were townspeople—students, bookkeepers, businessmen, teachers. They and their

Trends (Continued): Zionism

ancestors had had no contact with village life and agricultural problems for centuries. But they settled down in their new-old land, with its marsh and desert and rocks and its new strange climate of burning summer sun and torrential winter rains, determined to live on the soil and its produce. Along with some of the older residents, the "praying" Jews, they began to drain the marshes and till the soil of their ancient forebears. Many of them died of malaria. They made innumerable mistakes, but they learned from their experience.

The Jewish movement to rebuild Palestine did not become worldwide until the end of the nineteenth century. Oddly enough, the man who organized political Zionism on a world scale was himself a Westerner, an assimilated Jew, who knew very little about Judaism. His name was Theodor Herzl (1860–1904). He was born in Hungary and later settled in Vienna, Austria. There he worked for one of the leading newspapers. In 1891 he was appointed correspondent in Paris, and three years later was assigned to report the Dreyfus case.

Herzl was horrified by the anti-Jewish reaction of the street mobs, as well as that of high society, particularly the army and the church. It shattered his belief that assimilation had brought the Jews security. He thought deeply about the events around him, and the mob screaming "Down with the Jews!" in civilized Paris. And he arrived at the sad conclusion that the Gentile world would never really leave the Jews in peace.

As an assimilationist Jew Herzl did not know about earlier Jewish writings on the subject. He produced what he believed to be his own original solution in a book published in 1896 called *The Jewish State*.

These three words were the essence of Herzl's answer to the problem of anti-Semitism. In a Jewish state the Jews would be their own masters, no longer a minority at the mercy of a hostile Christian majority. To achieve this state, he argued in the book, the Jews must first obtain a charter from the sultan of Turkey, who then ruled Palestine, to permit the resettlement of the country as a Jewish state. It was also essential to get international recognition.

Herzl was a dynamic personality. A year later two hundred Jews answered his call to meet in Basel, Switzerland, for a congress to discuss his plans. They came from various parts of the world; they were Orthodox and Reform, rabbis and agnostics, businessmen, intellectuals, socialists and their opponents, students and workingmen. The congress ended with an accepted program: "to create for the Jewish people a home in Palestine secured by public law." In Basel, in 1897, modern political, as distinct from religious, Zionism was born.

Tirelessly, Herzl traveled from one European capital to another seeking to gain approval from governments and influential people. But the first problem was to obtain the charter from the sultan. And the sultan firmly refused. Not even Herzl's promise of millions of pounds for his empty treasury could move him.

Trends (Continued): Zionism

Turkey at the time had very little left of its great spirit of the sixteenth century. It still ruled vast territories, but its administration was corrupt and bankrupt, and world opinion had nicknamed it "the sick man of Europe." Jews under Turkish rule no longer enjoyed their earlier greatness. In fact, Jews under Moslem rule in the nineteenth century suffered from extreme discrimination, although they were spared the massacres of czarist Russia.

In North Africa, they had to live in the *mellah*, the Arab equivalent of the ghetto. In Yemen, they were actively persecuted. In Persia, they were treated as religiously impure. When it rained, Jews were not allowed in the streets in case their uncleanliness should wash off onto good Moslems. Now and then there were even forced conversions to Islam.

It soon became obvious that there was no hope of success from Herzl's efforts with the sultan. The British government offered him the British-ruled Sinai Peninsula on the southern borders of Palestine for Jewish settlement. But a commission went out to investigate and found the area unsuitable, almost entirely desert. Later, the British suggested Uganda in East Africa. Herzl himself felt rather inclined to accept this, as there seemed no hope of Palestine. But his more traditionally-minded colleagues, led by a man named Chaim Weizmann considered this a betrayal of the eighteen-hundred-year-old dream that only Palestine could fulfill. Herzl had to give in, and the Uganda idea fell through, too.

In 1904 Herzl died, worn out by overwork and constant traveling. His successors went on working for a world-recognized Jewish state in Palestine. But, at the same time, they also concentrated on piecemeal settlement—yet another Jewish village, suburb, school in Palestine, another few hundred Jews. These were meant to lay the foundations for the great day to come.

FROM AUTO-DA FE TO GAS CHAMBERS
· XX ·

IN THE MID-TWENTIETH CENTURY SIX MILLION JEWS, men, women, and children (one-third of the entire Jewish population of the world), were sent to their destruction. They died by torture, by gassing, by starvation, or by machine-gun fire. History books are full of the atrocities of past ages. But there are none, not even those of Genghis Khan, to match this deliberate annihilation of this astronomical number. It was a new crime, this mass destruction of a whole people, and a new word, *genocide*, had to be coined to describe it.

How could this happen in twentieth-century Europe? How could a madman like Adolf Hitler gain the active or passive support of one of the most advanced peoples of European civilization and thus smear the story of the human race?

Early in the twentieth century Germany was one of Europe's leading nations in industry, science, music, medicine, philosophy, and poetry. But psychologically, as a nation, Germany was a mere infant compared with most other European nations. It was one of the last countries to weld together its string of small independent states into one large, powerful, and united nation. And even before its complete unification it had demonstrated its strength to the outside world when, in 1871, it defeated proud France in the Franco-Prussian War.

The Germans took from defeated France the booty of the conqueror from time immemorial: land and money. And they took something else besides—an idea. They grabbed at the "Aryan superiority" theory of Count de Gobineau. They adapted it and Germanized it. They accepted that the Aryan race was superior to all others. More, they claimed that the elite among the Aryans could only be the Germans. For they had just *defeated* the French.

With this went the other part of the theory that the Semitic peoples were lowest in the ranks of humanity and that the Jews were the lowest even of these. For they were *destructive*.

In France itself, Gobineau's ideas had never struck deep roots. After the Dreyfus case and the defeat of the influential anti-Semites within the church, the army, and society generally, this idea of Jewish "racial" inferiority had almost disappeared. It lingered on as a talking point in the privacy of some salons but it was rarely aired in public.

It was quite different in Germany where the idea that the Germans were the salt of the earth, the "master race," was sweet music to the German soul. So was the other part of the theory that the Jews were destructive. It seemed obvious that everything good in Germany, therefore, must be the work of German Aryans. And everything bad and rotten in German life could only be the doing of the Jews.

The flaw in the theory, of course, was that Jews did in fact succeed in every walk of life in Germany. However, some writers, preachers, and politicians argued that the Jews could only have succeeded by fraud—by swindling honest German Aryans.

In 1881 an Anti-Semitic League had been established. It collected 255,000 signatures to a petition demanding that the government restrict Jewish activities and cut down their equality. Occasionally, street mobs would attack Jewish passers-by. Some people discarded even the Christian religion because it was Jewish and non-Aryan in origin. Others simply claimed that Jesus had been an Aryan from Gaul, not a Jew from Galilee.

It was not long before the Germans took this idea about racial superiority and inferiority away from the politicians and mobs into the academic field. A German professor of history, a fanatical nationalist named Heinrich von Treitschke, twisted his lectures and writings to fit this most unscientific idea. When his students at the university became schoolteachers and university lecturers themselves, they spread Treitschke's theories and his slogan "The Jews are our misfortune!" in other German universities and schools.

By the early twentieth century the young, unified nation of eighty million Germans—hardworking, intelligent, obedient to authority—had thoroughly digested their steady diet of "We are the master race." Active preparation and training for new conquests increased. War became inevitable and broke out in 1914 —World War I.

There were moments during that war when it looked as if Germany was going to win. If the United States had not come in to tip the scales against it, it probably would have done so. There were no nuclear bombs then and comparatively few air raids on civilians in towns. But by the time the war ended in November 1918 the fighting had pretty nearly annihilated the young men of Europe.

The slaughter of war was followed by the economic misery of peace. Economic planning had hardly been heard of. The ideas of social welfare and social security were still in their infancy.

Even the conquering countries had great unemployment with attendant poverty and hardship. In Germany, which had lost the war, things were infinitely worse. Year after year the German government had to pay out large sums of money to the victors, as war reparations and for the upkeep of occupation troops on German territory.

From Auto-da Fe to Gas Chambers

Worse still was the shattered national pride. They, the great German "master race," had been vanquished. Large slices of their land had been taken away from them. The holy soil of the Fatherland was polluted by the boots of enemy soldiers. Something had gone wrong. Somebody must be to blame.

The Germans were in agony. They longed for a Messiah, and they did not have to wait long before their false Messiah appeared—Adolf Hitler, attended by his Nazi "prophets." He came with no new ideas, no fresh theories, no fiery chariots from heaven. All the ideas and the practices he needed were there already, deeply rooted in the Germans. He merely had to bring them out into the open, canalize and develop them.

Hitler assured the Germans of something that they had secretly begun to doubt. They *were*—they would always remain—the "master race." Only a stab in the back by the destructive Jews, the enemy within, had snatched the victory from them. To save the situation it was only necessary to get rid of the Jews. Then Hitler would lead the German people to their glory and they would rule the world in the greatest empire it had ever known, an empire that would last a thousand years.

The Germans were convinced. After years of suffering, their redeemer had appeared at last. The Jews *were* their misfortune; they had always been— "Christ killers" during the Crusades, "well poisoners" in later slaughters. Now they must be punished for the stab in the back that had brought defeat. There were only six hundred thousand Jews among eighty million Germans.

Thousands of them had died in the war, fighting for the Fatherland. Many others had been decorated for bravery. Jewish scientists had made great contributions to the German war effort. But these were nothing but statistics against the deepest emotions of a bitterly wounded national pride.

Hitler seized upon Treitschke's words "The Jews are our misfortune!" as a slogan and made it ring from one end of Germany to the other. Muckraking in the pages of medieval church regulations, he found enough material to make life for Jews a misery. They were forbidden to mix with Aryans. They were to be dismissed from their offices—in government, in hospitals, in universities, in publishing—from any place where they had to deal with "real" Germans. Jews were not to employ Aryan servants. They were to wear yellow badges so that Aryans could recognize them at a glance. Hitler declared that any German who had one Jewish grandparent was himself Jewish.

Hitler was still frightened of the Jews, however—of the spiritual germs of brotherhood with which they had been infecting the world. This idea, more than any foreign armies, was what might stand in the way of German conquest. The Jews had to be wiped out. To Hitler and his Nazis, Christianity was no better than Judaism. It was a Jewish invention, and it preached love.

How, with this chain of love dragging at its heels, could the German people go forward with their great

From Auto-da Fe to Gas Chambers

task? Hitler could not wipe out Christianity completely with one blow, as he planned to do to the Jews and Judaism. What he could do, and did, was to reeducate German youth away from Christianity, back to the ancient German war gods, Wotan and Thor.

In September 1939, Hitler plunged the world into its second great war. He overran one country after another until he had nearly the whole of Europe. (Switzerland, Sweden, Spain, and Turkey were allowed to remain neutral.) Britain was fighting for survival, and Russia, of which the Germans had already swallowed an enormous chunk, was writhing in agony.

In every country Hitler conquered, one of his first acts was the systematic annihilation of its Jews. Only in one occupied country did this fail. In Denmark, when the occupying German forces ordered the Jews to wear the yellow badge, the king and all the court declared that they would wear it, too. And later, when the Nazis were getting ready to deport Danish Jews to the gas chambers in Poland, Gentile Danes, at enormous risk to themselves, managed to smuggle nearly all of the Jews across the sea to safety in neutral Sweden. In Amsterdam, Holland, too, half the Gentile population put on the yellow badges, in sympathy with their Jewish countrymen.

The Jews in the countries under German occupation were, if anything, more helpless than they had been during the medieval massacres. They were a handful against a multitude. In the twentieth century, however, the enemy was not an undisciplined mob but one of the best organized war machines of the day. And there could be no escape into baptism now.

In a few places the Jews did put up a fight. Like their blinded ancestor Samson in the hands of the Philistines, they felt that if they had to die, at least they would take some of the enemy with them. One of these pockets of Jewish resistance, the last-ditch fight of the Warsaw ghetto, has become part of the history of World War II.

The Germans had herded about half a million Jews inside the Jewish quarter of Warsaw, the Polish capital. They were half-starved, overcrowded, and plagued by all kinds of disease. From time to time the authorities would round up those useless to the German war effort —the children, the sick, the old—and march them off to cattle trucks bound for the death camps.

When there were only forty thousand of them left, these ghetto Jews, with some small arms and explosives they had managed to smuggle in, began to fight back. They held out for nearly three months, inflicting many casualties. In the end, of course, the mighty German war machine reduced the ghetto to rubble. Of the forty thousand Jews only a few escaped through the sewers.

Determined to establish the Germans permanently as the "master race" over a world of slaves, the Nazis also liquidated the non-Jewish intellectuals, teachers, writers, and other leading spirits among the conquered peoples who might dream of rebellion. They were particularly vigorous with this policy among the Poles

From Auto-da Fe to Gas Chambers

and the Russians, for these belonged to the Slav "race," another inferior people, though not as low as the Jews.

It looked very much as if Hitler was really going to succeed in turning the world into the Germans' "Promised Land." Then history repeated itself. The United States came in against the Fascist nations and tipped the scales again. Nazi Germany was crushed in 1945.

By then fifty million people had lost their lives. Of these, six million were Jews. They were helpless victims, deliberately exterminated. More Jews by the thousands died in the battlefields, fighting Nazism in the armies of the United States, Russia, Britain, France, Belgium, Holland, Poland, Yugoslavia, and Greece. There had been only sixteen million Jews in the world before 1939. More than a third of them fell, martyrs for the universal Jewish God to Wotan and Thor, the ancient pagan gods of Germany.

THE SOUND OF THE MESSIAH'S FOOTSTEPS
·XXI·

BY THE END OF WORLD WAR II THE GERMANS' FALSE Messiah had inflicted untold suffering on the rest of the world. He had also left his "master race" bleeding as it had never bled in all its history. Millions of Germany's youth lay buried under the boiling sands of Africa, the arctic snows of Russia, and the fields of Western Europe.

The vast wartime industry of Germany, fed by slave labor from all over occupied Europe, now lay devastated. Many German cities were heaps of rubble. Large slices of the new German Empire had been torn away. From these outposts, millions of German refugees fled to the Fatherland to swell the numbers of homeless widows and orphans.

The Sound of the Messiah's Footsteps

However, the world had no tears for the Germans. They had wanted their Messiah not to deliver them from suffering, but to hand over the rest of the world to them as slaves or as vermin to be destroyed. They had staked everything on the venture and lost.

The Messiah for whom the Jews had prayed for two thousand years, however, was universal. Their Messiah was coming not just to deliver the Jews from suffering and to restore Palestine to them. He was going to destroy evil throughout the world, so that the righteous of all nations could enjoy peace and justice for ever.

The Jews had always believed that the Messiah would appear only at their darkest hour. An early rabbi had even prayed: "Let Messiah come, but let me not be alive when he does." There could hardly have been a darker hour than that of the martyrdom of six million Jews under the Nazis.

After it, at last, came the sound of one footfall of Messiah. After nineteen hundred years of prayer, Palestine *was* restored to the Jews. The second footstep is yet to come. Evil has not disappeared from the world. Justice and peace do not yet reign supreme. And still, in some countries, the Jews wait for deliverance from suffering. Even the *newborn* Jewish nation in Palestine is beset by enemies who have sworn to destroy it. So the Jews go on praying for another footstep.

The rebirth of the Jewish people as an independent nation in its ancient homeland, after nearly two thousand years of exile, is an unparalleled phenomenon. It is difficult to pinpoint the exact moment when Jewish nationhood was reborn. Perhaps it was when the first "modern" Jewish villages in Palestine were established at the end of the nineteenth century. Perhaps it was when the Zionist Organization was founded in 1897. Perhaps it was in 1917 when Britain undertook to help build up a Jewish national home in Palestine. Or perhaps it was in 1923 when the League of Nations gave Palestine to Britain with a mandate to carry out its promise to the Jews. Or perhaps it was November 1947 when the U.N. voted for an independent Jewish state in a partitioned Palestine. But the official birthdate of Jewish nationhood, the one the world recognizes, is May 15, 1948, when the Jews in Palestine proclaimed an independent Israel. All these events were so interwoven and dependent on one another that none could have happened without the preceding one. They were really all part of one great historic moment.

The British promise to assist with the establishment of a Jewish national home is universally known as the Balfour Declaration. It was the result of several factors. One of them was the passion for the Bible that had made the British people familiar with the prophecies of the return of Jewish exiles to Palestine. This had produced a large number of non-Jewish writers and politicians in Britain who were "Zionists" even before Jewish political Zionism was born. The Victorian novelist George Eliot centered her book *Daniel Deronda* on this theme.

The Sound of the Messiah's Footsteps

On the more practical side, Britain and her Allies in World War I had been desperately trying to persuade the United States to come in on their side and save them from possible defeat by the Germans. The influential German-American community was campaigning against this. It was hoped that the Balfour Declaration would enlist support from American Jews. Until then, they had been rather cool toward the Allies, which included czarist Russia.

Thousands of leaflets announcing the Balfour Declaration were dropped by aircraft wherever there were large Jewish settlements, from Poland to the Black Sea and in Germany and Austria, too. The Germans and their Turkish allies immediately began work on a similar promise. But by the time they had agreed on it, the British were well on the way to conquering Palestine.

Another factor was the invention of an important, new explosive for the British war effort by Chaim Weizmann, a professor of chemistry at the University of Manchester in England. His invention brought him into contact with British leaders in and out of the government. It gave him the chance to explain Zionism to people who were both grateful to him and in a position to help.

Some statesmen, too, looked ahead to victorious peace, with Britain extending its empire even farther. Palestine, in its highly strategic position so near the then-vital Suez Canal route to India and beyond, would be more safely held if it was settled by people who were grateful to Britain, as well as dependent on it for their own security.

Jews all over the world greeted the British promise as the hour of deliverance. The British Foreign Minister, Lord Balfour, was regarded as the Messiah's messenger. Jewish women gave their jewelry—even their wedding rings—to the newly established Redemption Fund for the rebuilding of Palestine. Thousands of Jews volunteered for the Jewish battalions, which were to fight for the liberation of Palestine from the Turks. They were the first organized Jewish soldiers on Palestinian soil for eighteen centuries.

The first American Jewish Congress was convened in Philadelphia in December 1918 to "formulate a program for the protection of Jewish civil and ethnic rights in Europe to be presented at the Peace Conference in Versailles." Golda Meir, then twenty years old, was one of the delegates. This congress also adopted a resolution favoring the establishment of a Jewish homeland in Palestine.

Excluding the Crusading period, in the twelve hundred years since the Arabs captured it from the Byzantines, Palestine as a separate country had simply dropped out of world history. Only in the Jewish mind, and in its association with Jews as well as with Christianity in the minds of Gentiles, was it still very much alive.

Politically, economically, scientifically, philosophically, and artistically, Palestine had become a forsaken

The Sound of the Messiah's Footsteps

corner of the world. Apart from the Jewish Cabalists at Safed, it contributed nothing during this period. Its impoverished and disease-ridden inhabitants had no energy to learn from the progress of humanity. For all this time it had been a derelict stretch of land, sometimes part of one country or empire, sometimes of another, under the Byzantines, the Persians, the Arabs, the Mongols and the Turkish Ottoman Empire. The rocks of the Judean desert, the sands of the coastal plain, the malaria-producing marshes and lakes combined to decimate the population by disease and starvation. It was as if destiny itself had deliberately kept the country half-empty, waiting for the Jews to come back.

When Britain finally conquered the whole of Palestine in 1918, there was a sudden and dramatic change. It came to life again as a separate political unit, recognized as such by the rest of the world. And the Jews, encouraged by the promises of Britain and the newly formed League of Nations, determined to go back to their ancient soil and turn the wilderness it had become into a land flowing again with milk and honey.

At the time of the British conquest, Palestine's total population was seven hundred thousand, about that of a medium-sized modern American town. Of these fifty-eight thousand were Jews, seventy-four thousand were Christians, and the rest, more than half a million, were Moslems. There had been twice as many Jews before the war. But the Turks had expelled many of them because they were Russian, French, or British subjects, and others had left to escape the brutality and corruption of the Turkish authorities during the last years of their dying empire.

The British introduced into the country the first sound, healthy, experienced, and honest administration it had had for two thousand years. The scene seemed set for uninterrupted prosperity.

Thousands of new Jewish settlers arrived. They drained swamps. They built hill terraces. They planted millions of trees in a large-scale reforestation plan for the denuded country. And they built for themselves sound health and education services.

Therefore, the equally efficient health and education services of the British were free to concentrate on the welfare of the Arabs. Arab babies, who in the past had tended to die in their first year from inadequate feeding or dysentery, could now live to healthy adulthood. With mosquitoes controlled and marshland drained, malaria was conquered and Arab adults could look forward to living longer. There was work and prosperity, and the good tidings spread to Arabs in neighboring countries. These people, too, began to stream into Palestine.

The British-Jewish honeymoon was, however, a very short one. Soon after the British conquest Haj Amin-al-Husseini, a member of one of the leading Jerusalem Moslem families, which had held more or less feudal powers over the Arab peasants and workers, began to stir up violent agitation against the Balfour Declaration.

The Sound of the Messiah's Footsteps

His influence was immensely increased when the British later maneuvered to make him religious head (Mufti) of the Jerusalem Moslems.

To begin with, the Arabs in the neighboring countries were not particularly interested in this Palestine problem. They were enjoying their new freedom from centuries of Turkish oppression. They were also busily campaigning to convert their semi-independence, under British or French Trusteeship granted by the League of Nations, into complete independence. In the early stages they did almost exactly what Balfour had pleaded with them to do.

"I hope," he said, "they will remember that it is *we* who have established the independent Arab sovereignty of the Hejaz [now Saudi Arabia]. I hope they will remember that is is *we* who desire in Mesopotamia [now Iraq] to prepare a way for the future of a self-governing, autonomous Arab State. And I hope that, remembering all that, they will not grudge that small notch—for it is no more geographically, whatever it may be historically—that small notch in what are now Arab territories being given to the people who, for all these hundreds of years, have been separated from it."

Balfour's words applied equally to Syria and Lebanon, which had been put under a French mandate by the League of Nations, with a view to eventual independence. And Egypt, too, although still under British occupation, was well on the way to autonomy.

Soon after the war Faisal, who was the son of the

king of the Hejaz and who became first king of Iraq, made an agreement with Chaim Weizmann on the basis of the Balfour Declaration. The "small notch" of Palestine was to be developed by the Jews, while the Arabs would reconstruct their own lands.

Unfortunately, the vision of Balfour and other great British statesmen was now taken over by officialdom, which was in charge of making the dream become reality. There was an immediate change in the wind. Many influences had been at work against the Jews. Above all, there was the need to protect the British Empire, which extended then to the subcontinent of India and to Singapore. The Middle East lay astride the vital route to these outposts as well as to Australia and New Zealand, also part of the empire. In addition, Britain was becoming increasingly dependent on the oil fields it had been developing in Iraq.

It was, therefore, vital that the Middle East be made secure against any disturbance. Looking ahead, officials saw that the Balfour Declaration could create that very disturbance if the Arabs all over the Middle East moved to anti-Zionism. Against that possibility, they made a simple calculation—the few thousand Jews of Palestine against the many millions of Arabs in the Middle East. To this they added the millions of non-Arab Moslems in India and other parts of the empire, who might also become involved one day and declare themselves against a Jewish Palestine. The answer was plain. Balfour's argument that Palestine was a "notch" had been turned into a logical conviction *against* Zionism.

The Sound of the Messiah's Footsteps

The result was a long process of whittling down the great dream. A "Jewish national home," it was argued, did not mean a "Jewish state." Nor was the promise of a Jewish national home *in* Palestine meant to refer to the *whole* of Palestine.

So the mandated territory of Palestine was cut into two sections: east of the Jordan River and west of the Jordan. The Balfour Declaration was to apply only to the latter. The other two-thirds of the country, east of the Jordan, was renamed Transjordan, and given to Abdullah, another son of King Husein of the Hejaz.

Arab riots in Palestine were followed by restrictions on Jewish immigration. Having gotten a little of what they wanted, the Arabs rioted again in hopes of getting more. The Jews defended themselves with an underground military organization. The British impartially dealt out punishment to attackers and defenders alike.

On the Day of Atonement in 1929, beside the Western, or "Wailing," Wall of the ancient Jewish Temple in Jerusalem, a Jew signaled the end of prayers by the traditional blowing of a ram's horn trumpet, or *shofar*. The *mufti* of the Jerusalem Moslems protested that in doing this the Jews had broken the rules, which said only that they could continue to pray by the Western Wall as they had always done. The *mufti* claimed that they had never attempted to blow a *shofar* there before.

A rumor started, which spread rapidly to the farthest Arab villages, that the Jews had attacked the Mosque of Omar, one of the most holy of Moslem buildings, which had been built by the first Moslem conquerors inside the original Temple area.

This was completely untrue. But the Arabs immediately fell on vulnerable Jewish settlements throughout the country. Most of these were able to defend themselves. But Hebron, south of Jerusalem, had a tiny Jewish community of Talmudic students and scholars, who wanted to spend their lives near the traditional burial place of the Patriarchs Abraham, Isaac, and Jacob. There the Arabs, although they had been on excellent terms with the Jews for centuries, rose in a barbaric massacre, hacking scores of them to pieces.

After this the British imposed further restrictions on Jewish immigration and purchase of land. But because of strong protest by Jews and by the League of Nations, as well as by some British statesmen, these restrictions were withdrawn.

After Hitler came to power in Germany in 1933, Jewish immigration into Palestine increased. The Arabs protested and in 1936 broke into open rebellion in which the British as well as the Jews were attacked. For the first time, too, Arabs from outside Palestine were actively involved. Syrian Arabs came to fight side by side with the Palestinian Arab guerrillas.

It was 1939 before the rebellion was near to being crushed. By that time Britain was hastily getting ready for the war with Hitler that had been threatening for years. It was more important than ever to secure the lines of communication with India and the Far East.

The Sound of the Messiah's Footsteps

To safeguard Arab loyalty it seemed essential to remove any grievances.

To do this, officialdom produced exactly the event it had feared twenty years earlier—the involvement of all Middle Eastern Arabs in the affairs of Palestine. The British government called to a conference, which was to decide the future of Palestine, not only representatives of the Palestinian Arabs and of the Jewish Agency, but also the leaders of the Arab countries.

This conference resulted in a British White Paper, or official decision, which to all intents and purposes stopped immigration and land purchase by Jews. Many members of the British Parliament, among them Winston Churchill, called it a "breach of a solemn obligation." The League of Nations, too, refused to accept the new policy. And the Jews of Palestine declared that they would fight to the last man against a policy that would make the Jewish national home the only country in the modern world where Jews were to be deprived of the right to buy land and pushed back into a kind of ghetto.

However, when World War II broke out later the same year, the Palestinian Jews announced that they would fight Hitler as if there were no White Paper, but would fight the White Paper in Palestine as if there were no war. Thousands volunteered to join the Jewish units of the armed services, which the British had formed in Palestine. They fought on almost every front.

Once the war was over the Jews began their own guerrilla warfare against the British in Palestine. At the same time they smuggled in thousands of survivors from the death camps instead of the prewar hundreds. The Arabs stood back, contented onlookers in this bitter struggle between the British and the Jews.

In 1947, thirty years after the Balfour Declaration, Britain asked the United Nations, successors to the League of Nations, for a decision on future policy. By the necessary two-thirds majority, the U.N. decided to partition Palestine west of the Jordan River. Its population of around 750,000 Jews and 1,300,000 Moslem and Christian Arabs were to live in two independent states, one Arab and one Jewish.

The British refused to accept the decision, and announced that by May 14, 1948, they would give up the mandate and withdraw from the country. Thus ended the British-Jewish partnership. Ironically, it also produced the fulfillment of the Balfour Declaration—a Jewish national home in Palestine.

THE WANDERER GOES HOME
· XXII ·

THE JEWS HAD ALWAYS BELIEVED THAT THEIR DEliverance would come by a miracle. But there was little in the rebirth of the Jewish nation in Palestine that was obviously miraculous.

Miracle or no, on May 14, 1948, a day before the last of the British officials and soldiers had left Palestine, the Jews declared their independence in the territory that the U.N. had allotted them. And so Israel was born 1,878 years after Judea had been destroyed by the Roman Titus.

The next day Egypt, Syria, Transjordan, Lebanon, and Iraq invaded it. They all had trained armies with modern weapons. Most of them were members of the

United Nations, and forbidden under its Charter to wage war. Day-old Israel was the U.N.'s baby. But the U.N. did not send troops to protect Israel. It did not even call for sanctions against the Arabs. Nor did it pass any formal resolution condemning the Arab invasion.

On the battlefield, however, Israel was steadily gaining on the Arabs. There was little of the supernatural about this. The Arab states were bitterly jealous of one another, each planning to annex Palestine for itself after victory. Soon it too became obvious that the Arab armies were badly led, most of the Arab soldiers did not have their hearts in the war—after all *they* were not fighting for their homes and national survival.

But the Jews had no choice. After almost nineteen hundred years of persecution, after the martyrdom of six million Jews by the Nazis, the Israelis were determined to sell their lives, if they had to, at the highest price possible. With their backs to the Mediterranean Sea, and every other border lined by hostile Arabs, they fought—and they advanced.

The U.N. called for a thirty-day truce, threatening both sides with sanctions if they did not call a cease-fire. Thirty days afterward, fighting started again. This time the Israelis pushed the Arabs back far beyond the boundaries the United Nations had laid down. At this the U.N. called for another truce.

The cease-fire was followed by an Armistice Agreement between Israel and all its Arab enemies except one —Iraq. The agreement was signed after much negotiation between the two sides with Ralph Bunche of the

The Wanderer Goes Home

U.N. as mediator. All parties undertook to follow up with a permanent peace settlement, and in the meantime to avoid any warlike action against one another.

The Israelis had been angry and disillusioned to see that neither the U.N. nor any of its member nations had helped them when the whole world expected them to be wiped out in a matter of days. But as events turned out it gave them enormous confidence to know that they had won their war single-handed.

All the same, they had heavy casualties, and they had lost the walled Old City of Jerusalem. There were ten thousand casualties in a population of less than a million. It was as if Great Britain had lost half a million people. There were very few families in Israel that had nobody to mourn for.

The Old City of Jerusalem, within its medieval walls, was in the hands of Abdullah, the ruler of Transjordan. He now became king of the newly named state of Jordan, which included the Arab-occupied parts of Palestine west of the Jordan River and the walled Old City of Jerusalem. The Jews of the Old City had put up a strong fight against an overwhelming majority, the Arab inhabitants and King Abdullah's army. They were shelled without respite and could get little help from Jewish Jerusalem outside the walls. For this too was besieged, cut off from the rest of the Jewish state by Arab artillery trained on the steep and winding main road to the coast. These Jews, too, were shelled and sniped at and starved for weeks on end.

For the first time since the Crusades, Jews had been

driven out of old Jerusalem. There was not a single Jew anywhere near the Western Wall, the symbol of the Jews' love for their country. The synagogues in the Jewish Quarter that had survived the war had been razed to the ground. And the Jews were also cut off from their ancient cemetery on the Mount of Olives, with its monuments to the Prophet Zachariah and Absalom, son of David.

But the sad-happy Israelis now set their sights on the future. A provisional government was formed, with David Ben-Gurion as Prime Minister and Defense Minister. Later Dr. Chaim Weizmann, the aged Zionist leader, was elected first President of the reborn Jewish state. Basic to its constitution is the Law of Return, by which every Jew everywhere can claim the right to settle in the country.

The Jews then worked energetically to turn the desert country within their boundaries into fertile fields. The people who had kept faith with the land were reunited with the land that had kept faith with them. Shiploads of Jews arrived from every corner of the world. Dark-skinned Jews from India and African Ethiopia mingled with immigrants from the Americas and from Europe.

Above all, there were three quarters of a million from the Arab countries. The entire Jewish community of Yemen was transported to Israel by an immense airlift. Most of these people were so primitive that they were terrified to board the buses that came to meet them. The airplanes they took for granted because of the

The Wanderer Goes Home

ancient prophecy that the exiles would return "on the wings of eagles."

About a hundred thousand came from Iraq, more than double those who returned from ancient Babylonia after King Cyrus gave permission to rebuild Jerusalem and its Temple. Now, only a few thousand who felt unable to part with their property remained in Iraq. Thus came the end of the 2,500-year-old chapter of the Babylonian Jews. It had been a glorious chapter very nearly up to the Moslem period. The role it had played in the development of Judaism is so important that Jewish life everywhere is still under its influence.

Jews from other Arab countries, too, flocked to Israel —from Syria, Egypt (another ancient and influential center of Jewish life), Lebanon, Morocco, Tunis, Algeria, Libya. Many of them arrived in Israel with little more than the clothes they were wearing, but the Israelis welcomed them as much as they welcomed affluent Jews from the West. Every effort was made to house and feed them and train them for their new life.

At the same time Israel also took care of its quarter of a million Arab citizens. They advanced economically, educationally, and in their freedom, until they were much better off than the Arabs in any of the Arab countries.

The half million Arabs who had left their homes and villages in the new Israel when war broke out and fled into the bordering states met a different fate. Some had gone because they believed the promise of the

Arab governments that the war would last only a few days, after which they could return not only to their own homes but to those of the Jews as well. Others had simply fled before the advancing Israelis during the war. Almost at once they embarked on a life of misery. Instead of being taken to the houses and properties the Jews had abandoned when they fled to Israel, they were left to linger and multiply in refugee camps.

They became political pawns in a new type of war that the Arab states had embarked on almost before the ink was dry on their signatures to the Armistice Agreement. Instead of peace there were warlike acts as well as words. Israeli ships were not allowed passage through the Suez Canal, nor through the Gulf of 'Aqaba to the Israeli port of Eilat, its only outlet to the East and Far East. Even ships of other nations carrying goods to or from Israel were forbidden to use the canal.

The 150,000 Arab refugees who had fled to the Gaza Strip, on the northeastern corner of the Sinai Peninsula, which remained under Egyptian occupation, were not allowed to go into Egypt proper and begin a new life. Jordan would have preferred to absorb the refugees in the camps there and give them full equality with its own citizens. Its good intentions were blocked by propaganda from other Arab governments, demanding the return of the refugees to Israel.

In 1955 Russia began to arm Egypt, at first through her satellite Czechoslovakia and later directly. Trained Egyptian commando units were sent over the border

The Wanderer Goes Home

in constant raids directed chiefly against the Israeli civilian population. Bombs were thrown into crowded areas such as marketplaces, theaters and even schools, with many casualties among Israeli men, women, and children. Israel retaliated with counter-raids into the Egyptian-held Gaza Strip.

But Egyptian commando raids continued. This led ultimately to the Sinai War of 1956 in which Israel captured the Gaza Strip and advanced on Egyptian Sinai, coming to a halt a few miles east of the Suez Canal. This invasion was timed to coincide with an invasion of Egypt on the west side of the canal by British and French troops. Their aim was to restore the canal to the international company that had owned and administered it until Egypt took over and nationalized it a few months earlier.

The United Nations, however, threatened sanctions unless the British, French, and Israelis withdrew completely. President Eisenhower of the United States promised that if Israel withdrew, the United States would protect the passage of all ships, including Israel's, through the Gulf of 'Aqaba. The United Nations raised a peace-keeping force to be stationed between Israel and Egypt to prevent the commando raids. A similar unit was stationed at Sharm el Sheikh on the southern corner of Sinai, which controls entry to the Gulf of 'Aqaba.

The commando raids continued, however—now from Jordan and Syria where there were no peace-keeping

U. N. troops. Israel retaliated. Raids and counter-raids were almost incessant. Arab leaders talked openly of war, and Egypt, Syria, and Jordan united their armies under one command.

Then Egypt sent one hundred thousand troops into Sinai, and ordered the U.N. peace-keeping force out of Sharm el Sheikh. Egypt reoccupied it and closed the Gulf of 'Aqaba to Israeli shipping. The noose tightened around Israel's neck, and its strangulation seemed inevitable. But no nation offered help. The U.N. did not raise a force to aid Israel, nor did it even threaten the Arabs with sanctions if they went to war.

In Israel itself, those who feared defeat steeled themselves for another Masada on a gigantic scale. Israelis—even Arab Israelis—queued to donate blood for the coming emergency.

On June 5, 1967, the six-day war broke out. The U.N. ordered a cease-fire. By the end of a week the Arab countries had agree to it, and the shortest war in history was over. The Gaza Strip and the whole Sinai Peninsula were in the hands of the Israelis. The only Egyptian soldiers there were groups of forlorn men wandering in the hot sands of the desert, grateful to Israeli soldiers for a cup of water. The Egyptian tanks and guns were either burnt-out skeletons or booty for the Israelis. In Sharm el Sheikh Israel took over from the Egyptians, who had themselves taken over from the U.N. only a fortnight earlier.

Israel was equally victorious on its eastern front,

The Wanderer Goes Home

against Jordan and Syria. What was left of the Jordanian army rolled back across the Jordan River. Hebron and the entire Arab bulge west of the Jordan became Israeli-occupied territory. The walled Old City of Jerusalem was reunited with Jewish Jerusalem outside the walls.

In the northeast, the Israelis drove out the Syrians from their emplacements on the Golan Heights. For years the Jewish villages in the valley below had had to endure shellfire from the Heights whenever the Syrians felt like it. But the Israelis were now only forty miles away from Syria's capital, Damascus.

The Israelis held the east bank of the Suez Canal and the whole western shore of the Gulf of 'Aqaba. To the east they were on the west bank of the Jordan. These water frontiers were obviously more easily defended against invasion than artificial land frontiers. Tel Aviv and other densely populated Israeli areas could now have fifteen minutes' warning of a threatened air raid, instead of the prewar four minutes. And Cairo had four minutes where before it had had fifteen.

The new frontiers, oddly enough, were also shorter than the old ones. The previous land frontiers with Egypt, and even more those with Jordan, wove so crazily in and out that their combined length was nearly double that of a straight-line frontier.

Israel had lost 800 out of 2,250,000 Jewish Israelis—the equivalent of 17,000 out of the U.K. population. There was mourning for the dead, but also immense relief at the survival of the rest and the barely believable victory. More than all the military gains, the Israelis rejoiced over the capture of the walled Old City of Jerusalem, with its national shrine in the Western Wall.

For a time, too, Israel felt certain of its future. It seemed impossible that the Arabs would not be ready now for a permanent peace. The occupied Arab territories could be traded for peace and security. Israel had no ambitions for an empire. In any case, a permanent annexation of the conquered land would have meant the spiritual, if not physical, destruction of Israel. Already the 2,250,000 Israelis were becoming alarmed about the rapid birth rate of the Israeli Arabs as compared with the far smaller Jewish birthrate. To take in another million Arabs would soon turn the Israeli Jews into a minority in their own country.

For a few weeks it seemed as if the dream of peace would come true. Secret negotiations with Jordan were already far advanced. But in August 1967 the Russians promised Egypt a complete replacement of all the airplanes, tanks, and guns they had lost in the war. At once a large-scale airlift began to fly in the promised arms.

Later the same month all the Arab countries, not only Israel's neighbors but even Sudan and Algeria, met and decided on a formula: no recognition of Israel; no negotiations with Israel; no peace.

After that the cease-fire ordered by the U.N. was broken almost daily by the Egyptians and Jordanians. The Egyptians shelled Israeli military positions across the Suez Canal. The Jordanians shelled Israeli villages west of the Jordan, where children had been going to bed in underground shelters, some of them ever since they were born. The Arabs were also spending millions of pounds from their oil royalties to train and equip Arab refugees, or rather their grown-up sons, as guerrilla bands to cross the borders into Israel for sabotage and murder. Through extensive propaganda they circulated some anti-Israeli libels as absurd as the medieval libel that the Jews had caused the Black Death.

Meanwhile, the Israelis continued to look after their future security. They were determined not to give up an inch of the conquered land without a permanent peace settlement. Although they disliked the role of occupying troops, they could not afford to abandon the extra security this gave them or its usefulness as a bargaining counter.

Behind their military shield the Israelis continued building up their ancient land as if there were no threat of a new war. They went on absorbing thousands of Jews who arrived to fulfill their ancient dream. They planted new forests. They expanded the economy, making room for thousands still getting ready to come, and perhaps for the flood of Russian Jews waiting for their government to open the locked exits.

THE DIASPORA AFTER HITLER
·XXIII·

THE REBIRTH OF THE JEWISH PEOPLE IN AN INDEPENdent Israel still leaves about ten million Jews outside—in the Diaspora. How do they live now? What does the future hold for them?

Their lives, too, have undergone a transformation that would have been unbelievable up to the end of World War II in 1945. Hitler and his Nazis had every detail of their "final solution" of the Jewish problem planned—to destroy every Jew in the world. The Nazi defeat brought anti-Semitism to the beginning of its end. The "final solution," in fact, seems to be advancing in the direction of removing, at long last, not the Jews but the age-old hatred of them.

The Diaspora After Hitler

The gas chambers bequeathed to the Christian world a new Cross, blazing with six million branches of the kinsmen of Jesus. The Christian world—not merely the Germans—felt responsible for all the past centuries that had led up to the gas chambers.

Anti-Semitism has become such a shocking word that some people accused of it have threatened legal action for libel.

The Catholic Church has at last officially declared Jews free of the accusation of deicide—'God-killing'. And although fear of the persecution of Christians in Arab countries has so far prevented the Pope from openly recognising the State of Israel, he had nevertheless received the Israeli Prime Minister in audience.

Even in Spain, the small Jewish community of about 10,000 are fully accepted into society. On the 16th December 1968 the Spanish Ministry of Justice issued a law legalising the existence of the Madrid Jewish Community. The document was presented to the Community's Vice-President, Samuel Toledano, a direct descendant of the Rabbi of Toledo who had received the expulsion order from Ferdinand and Isabella in 1492.

A handful of Jews settled in Spain early in this century. More arrived just before World War II. But the real revival of the Jewish community there began during the War itself, and it was the Spanish Government which started it. On 14th December 1943 it ordered the Spanish Embassy in Berlin to rescue a group of Sephardi Jews, descendants of the Spanish exiles, from the Bergen Belsen concentration camp. A first group of 162 arrived in Spain on February 9, 1944, and was followed soon afterwards by another 983.

Another act turning back the pages of history by Spain was the recent erection of a monument to Maimonides, the great medieval Jewish philosopher and physician, in his Spanish birthplace, Cordova.

As for the non-Catholic countries, it is enough to mention two examples of present-day attitudes to Judaism in Britain and in the U.S.A. The British Broadcasting Corporation, in its World Service, for a time ran a series of Hebrew prayers on Saturdays at the end of the News instead of the usual Christian prayers which are broadcast during the rest of the week. In the United States, a Rabbi takes part in the religious ceremonies of the inauguration of a new president, and *kasher* (ritually pure) food is provided for him.

Events like this seem hardly believable when one thinks of the dark age when the Jewish holy books were ceremonially burned, and, too often, Jews themselves were sacrificed to the flames of intolerance.

Of course, anti-Semitism has not yet disappeared from the face of the earth. Nearly two thousand years of teaching cannot be wiped out as quickly as that. There are still clubs that shut their doors to Jews and individual people who bar Jews socially. But even these, nowadays, hotly deny that anti-Semitism is the reason. For anti-Semitism can be camouflaged under the terms "anti-Israel" or "anti-Zionist." Both these terms have a

The Diaspora After Hitler

degree of respectability among well-meaning but innocent liberal-minded people who like to take the side of the underdog. In 1967 when it looked as if the Israelis were going to be annihilated by their Arab neighbors, these people campaigned against the Arabs. But Israel's unexpected victory, and its occupation of Arab territory with a population of a million Arabs, soon somehow transformed the hundred million inhabitants of fourteen Arab states into the "underdog." And many of the kindhearted liberals turned against Israel.

Some of the idealistic younger generation today believe the world's defects to be the result of Western civilization. To these young people, the Jews have become Westerners. They employ Western techniques and seek Western support and are to be condemned for this.

To those who dream of social equality and who follow the Communist lead, Zionism—up to November 29, 1947—was "a tool of British imperialism" because Russia said so. Then Russia voted for a Jewish state in partitioned Palestine and endorsed Zionism in a most impassioned speech to the U.N. Almost overnight, Zionism became a great humanistic ideal to those to whom Russia's word was law. In 1955 Russia again changed its view and armed the Arabs against Israel, which they now branded as a tool of *American* imperialism. These are some of the disguises of anti-Semitism.

The Jews outside Israel enjoy to the full their own complete freedom and equality. They are more numerous than the Jews in Israel, but this is nothing new. Before the destruction of the Jewish state in A.D. 70 there were already more Jews outside than inside.

The loyalty of these Jews is to the country in which they live. Often it is super-patriotic—somebody once said that the Jews are just like their non-Jewish neighbors, only more so. At the same time, they are happy about the realization of the ancient dream of Israel.

They are also proud of Israel's achievements. Their hearts glow when Israeli experts on agriculture are sent to advise and direct underdeveloped countries in Asia, Africa, and Latin America. Their cup of joy almost overflowed after the three military victories of Israel in its twenty years of existence. At last that insulting label "Coward!" had been wiped out. Through centuries of massacres and persecution, Jews were proud of the martyrdom of their families and friends. But they also longed for the chance to fight back—to be like the biblical Samson. The young postwar generation of Jews often felt half-ashamed of the six million Jews who went like sheep to the Nazi slaughter. After the Israeli victories a Jew could no longer be looked on as a coward or a cringer.

Because the Jews outside are both proud of Israel and grateful to it, they express this in their identification with Israel's problems, making its cause their own. Two thousand years ago, the Diaspora Jews paid a voluntary tax for the upkeep of the Temple in Jerusalem. Now, every year, Jews of the modern Diaspora pour out

The Diaspora After Hitler

generous donations to help with the resettlement of the endless flow of newcomers to Israel. They make every effort to visit Israel, just as their ancestors made pilgrimage to Jerusalem and the Temple.

Of course, this is not true of all Jews—there are the usual exceptions to prove the rule. There is a small sect of extremely orthodox Jews, in Israel as well as outside, who cling fanatically to the old hope of a heavenly Messiah. Unlike other orthodox Jews who rejoice in Israel while continuing to pray for the Messiah, these extremists, even within Israel itself, refuse to recognize the authority of their own state. Only the Messiah can proclaim the birth of Israel, they declare.

At the other extreme, there are a few ultra-assimilationists who, because of their denial of national attributes to the Jews, have gone over to a campaign against Israel. They fear that an independent Jewish state could result in an accusation against Jews everywhere of "double loyalty"—to their own country and to Israel. These people ignore similar cases, such as the love and devotion felt by large numbers of Scots and Irish living abroad for the land of their fathers.

This generally optimistic picture of the Jews in the present-day Diaspora is not true of all of it. Quite a sizable number are still oppressed and depressed. First, there are the few thousands still in the Arab countries. Their position, both physically and spiritually, is truly pitiful. In Syria and Iraq, Jews are barred from most employment and are allowed to draw only monthly sums from their bank accounts. Their movements are restricted, and at frequent intervals they have to report to the police. These are the lucky ones, the "free" Jews. Many others linger in jail on trumped-up charges. Some have been hanged, with great public pomp, accused of spying for Israel. None are allowed to leave the country.

A far larger number—about three million—in the Soviet Union suffer a variety of disadvantages. There is not the slightest resemblance in their physical condition to that of their fathers under the czars or to that of the Jews in Arab countries. Officially, they have equal rights with non-Jewish Russians. Anti-Semitic practices are punishable crimes. But spiritually today's Russian Jews are in a way worse off than their ancestors were under the czars. In a country that has declared war on all religion, the Jews lack religious teachers, rabbis, prayer books. Hebrew, as distinct from Yiddish, is officially frowned upon. Sympathy for Israel is taboo. The many Russian nations that make up the U.S.S.R. are free to express their national feelings and develop their own cultures, but the Jews are not. This is because Jewish nationalism is historically tied up with religion and because the Jewish national aspirations lie outside Soviet territory, in Israel. Since Russia, at present, is supporting the Arabs, any signs of goodwill toward Israel are politically discreditable. Russian Jews who refuse to be divorced either from

The Diaspora After Hitler

their religion or from their dream of Israel are, in another respect, worse off than their ancestors. They are quite simply not allowed to leave the country at all. In fact, Russian Jews today are safe and secure only when they cease to be Jews.

A certain amount of plain old-fashioned religious anti-Judaism still lingers on in a society that officially discarded Christianity in the early 1920's. Books attacking the Jewish religion in near-medieval terms have been published in Russia—and nothing is published without permission from the government. The ancient law "an eye for an eye, a tooth for a tooth" is still quoted as representing Judaism when the fact is that for thousands of years this has been interpreted by the rabbis to mean money compensation.

Crude modern anti-Semitism, too, appears on the surface in Communist Russia. In the persecution mania of his later years, Stalin was convinced that Jewish doctors were planning to poison him. Many Jewish doctors and intellectuals paid for his paranoia with their lives. A remark by a later premier, Khrushchev, to the Polish Communist leadership that there were too many Jews among them reverberated all over the world.

THE DIASPORA AFTER HITLER Jews in the U.S.A.
·XXIV·

THERE IS A TALMUDIC SAYING THAT GOD ALWAYS creates the antidote before He creates the disease. Columbus began his report to King Ferdinand of Spain on his historic expedition with a reference to Jewish suffering. "And thus, having expelled all the Jews from all your kingdoms and dominions, in the same month . . . your Highness commanded me that with a sufficient fleet, I should go to the said parts of India." Ferdinand and his queen, who had exiled the Jews, were also instrumental in the discovery of the very continent that later became a haven for many millions of exiles, oppressed Jews included.

Columbus himself is thought to have been of Jewish

The Diaspora After Hitler

descent. And his expedition was financed by a loan from two New Christians, Luis de Santagel and Gabriel Sanchez. In fact, there was only one "old" Christian among the people who planned the expedition, and even he had a New Christian wife. The first member of the expedition to set foot on American soil was Luis de Lorres, the interpreter, a Jew who was baptized just before sailing.

Columbus' discovery of the New World brought hope and excitement to the New Christians. They began to emigrate there in search of greater religious freedom. The Inquisition tried to stop this movement by insisting on a strict screening of all emigrants. But in spite of this many Marranos escaped and were soon to be found in all the new American settlements. Some of them were conquistadores in Mexico, and before long they controlled Mexican trade with Europe.

Unfortunately for these Marrano emigrants, side by side with the Spanish Army and the Spanish governor marched the Spanish clergy. In 1520, long before the official establishment of the Inquisition in Mexico, a Spanish soldier suspected of being a secret Jew was executed. There were many executions after this, and some Marranos were sent back to Spain to stand trial there.

In 1571 branches of the Inquisition were officially established in Mexico, and soon after in other parts of the New World as well. Not to be outdone by the extravagance in Spain, the Inquisition in Mexico carried out their *autos-da-fé* with much more pomp and ceremony than was the custom in Spain itself.

When the Dutch took Brazil from the Portuguese in 1620, Marranos threw off their disguise and began to form Jewish communities. But in 1654 when the Portuguese recaptured the colony, they had to flee to other American colonies under Dutch, French, or English rule. Jewish settlements sprang up all over the West Indies—in Jamaica, Curaçao, Barbados, for example.

One group of refugees from Brazil took ship for Dutch New Amsterdam. They ran into bad weather, and all except twenty-three were lost at sea. Those who reached New Amsterdam were forbidden by the local governor to own land, to trade with the Indians, or to take part in guard duties. Instead, they had to pay an extra tax. But Asher Levy, one of the survivors, put up a fight against the guard duty ruling and won. Very soon, the other restrictions were removed. By 1664, when New Amsterdam fell to the British, who renamed it New York, the Jews there had almost achieved equal rights with the other citizens. (In 1730 the first Jewish synagogue in North America was built in New York City.)

Jews also spread out to other colonies and were welcomed more in some places than in others. By 1658 there were fifteen Jewish families in the Rhode Island colony, founded in 1636 by the Puritan English clergyman Roger Williams. There, where the charter declared that "all men may walk as their conscience persuades them," they were most generously welcomed. Before long there was a thriving Jewish community in Newport, developing the whaling, soap, and candle industries. Later in the seventeenth century Jewish settlements sprang up in Pennsylvania, North and South Carolina, and Georgia.

In most of the colonies relations between Jews and Christians were excellent. By the middle of the eighteenth century there were even places where Jews contributed to the building fund for a church and the Christians to that for a synagogue.

In the War of Independence Jews fought against the English, some of them even converting their merchantships into warships. Others, however, fought with the English. In Newport, the Jewish families of Hart and Pollock were pro-British, and Rebecca Franks, a daughter of the merchant David Franks, was the toast of the British officers in Philadelphia. The Jewish merchants of Newport were very badly hit by the war and never recovered their original prosperity.

The Constitutional Convention of 1787 stated that "no religious test shall ever be required as a qualification to any office or public trust under the United States." And the First Amendment of 1789 added "Congress shall make no law respecting an establishment of religion or prohibiting the free exercise thereof." Thus American Jews were the first in any Christian country to become fully equal citizens with their Gentile neighbors.

American Jews have never had ghettos or massacres or expulsions. They continued their steady advance to prosperity without the setbacks of European Jews. The Jews of the United States contributed their full share to building the richest and strongest country in the world. No one grudged them either their contribution or their reward.

Few could deny, of course, that there is a lunatic fringe, such as the KKK or the tiny group of American Nazis. And deep in the hearts of many Gentile Americans there is still a greater or a lesser degree of anti-Jewish feeling. For, after nearly two hundred years of Americanization, the United States still has two distinct faces. To the rest of the world it is a united nation of two hundred million people. But inwardly it remains a mixture of innumerable large or small groups, divided by race, color, or religion. In the circumstances, it would be a miracle if the anti-Jewish prejudice of centuries were to vanish, so to speak, overnight.

As things stand, the five to six million United States Jews form the largest compact Jewish community in the world, as well as the most prosperous. It is double the size of the Jewish community in the Soviet Union and more than double the population of Israel. There has not yet been a Jewish President. But that does not diminish the Jewish community's importance. As a populous and prosperous section of a democracy, it helps to form government policy as regards Israel. It is difficult to imagine how far behind Israel would have been today, in its industry, finance, and defense,

The Diaspora After Hitler

without the help of American Jewry. Even in manpower, the U.S. Jewish community makes its small contribution, with a steady trickle of emigrants to Israel.

The United States—itself composed of many refugees and immigrants—helped to save the world twice over from enslavement by the "master race." They also poured out a vast treasure, the fruit of their labors in their new country, to feed and reconstruct the old countries.

Even if American help had not materialized during the wars, the Gentiles in Europe would still have been able to carry on some sort of existence. Crushed by the jackboots of the conquerors, with many killed or dying of starvation, there would still have been enough left to hope for another day.

For the Jews, however, things would have been very different. If the United States had not stepped in to help save Europe from Hitler, there would have been no Jews left in the Nazi empire. It is an odd coincidence that America was discovered in one of the Jews' darkest hours. In America a mighty nation was to arise to give succor to Jews in many other dark hours in their history.

GREAT BRITAIN
XXV

THE NEXT JEWISH COMMUNITY IN SIZE AND STANDING IS that of Great Britain and the other English-speaking countries which are or were part of the British Commonwealth (Canada, South Africa, Australia, New Zealand, Ireland and Rhodesia). There are about a million Jews in these countries, about half of them in Great Britain.

Earlier on, in discussing Jewish emancipation, there were fleeting references to what happened in Britain between the Cromwell-Menasseh ben Israel negotiations in the 1650's, and 1871 when the last restriction on Jews was lifted. In that period of over two centuries the Jews in Britain led a reasonably good life. Strong opposition did prevent Cromwell from granting an official Charter for Jewish settlement in Britain, and Menasseh ben Israel died 'heart-broken' because of it.

All the same, in a typically British compromise, Cromwell promised protection to the Jews already in the country, and to any newcomers, provided that they observed their religion in private and did not draw too much attention to their presence. And this lack of an official charter was possibly a blessing. At the Restoration, many of Cromwell's laws were repealed, and if the Lord Protector had made a law in favour of the Jews there would undoubtedly have been a great clamour for its abolition.

What happened in fact, however, was that Charles II wrote a note assuring the worried Jews that conditions for them would not be changed. Like Cromwell before him, Charles must have been acutely aware of the benefits the Jews had brought to Holland, and wished to see Jewish energy and enterprise directed towards the greater prosperity of Britain.

Moreover, as Jews did not *legally* exist in Britain, there could be no specific legal restrictions against them. They could live anywhere they liked, engage in most occupations, and mix freely with Gentile society. The few exceptions that did exist had nothing to do with any special anti-Jewish laws. They existed because of, first, the centuries-old practice of taking a Christian oath, which a Jew could not of course do. Secondly, the country had various restrictions directed mainly against

Christian dissenters, Roman Catholic or non-Conformist, from the Church of England, and these naturally affected Jews as well as Christians. Thirdly, there was the fact that for a considerable period the Jews in Britain, except for those born in the country, remained officially foreigners.

Thus Jews could not keep retail shops in the City of London, nor enter the legal profession. They could not stand for Parliament, nor be appointed to any public office. Oxford and Cambridge Universities were closed to Jewish students. And Jews could not give evidence in a court of law. The chief obstacle for them was this inability to take the oath 'on the true faith of a Christian' as the formula went.

Progress was slow, and Jewish disabilities were removed piecemeal. In 1723 an Act of Parliament permitted Jews to give evidence in Court without taking a Christian oath. In 1753 a Bill (the 'Jew Bill') was passed by Parliament, granting Jews who had lived in Britain for at least 3 years the right to apply for naturalisation. There was an anti-Jewish storm, and the year after the Bill was repealed.

The next major legal steps towards equality for British Jews had to wait until 1833, when Macaulay, the historian, in the Commons and the Duke of Sussex, sixth son of George III, in the Lords, introduced a Bill for Jewish Emancipation. It was passed by the Commons, but the Lords rejected it several times.

In the same year, however, Jews were admitted to the

Great Britain

Bar, and in 1835 they were allowed to become sheriffs of the Corporation of London, an office which then and now generally leads to a knighthood. Sir David Salomons was the first Jewish sheriff, and a relation of his, Sir Moses Montefiore, was the second. In 1845 Jews were permitted to occupy local government offices. A year later the Religious Opinion Relief Bill removed further disabilities for the Jews.

The right of Jews to sit in parliament was won only after a long-drawn-out battle. In 1847 the City of London returned Lionel de Rothschild to the House of Commons as their Member. But as he took his oath holding a copy of the Old Testament and omitting the phrase 'on the true faith of a Christian' he was not allowed to take his seat.

In 1851 David Salomons was elected member for Greenwich, took the oath in the same way, took his seat and voted. For this he was fined £500. He persisted in voting, and paid two more fines before he gave up.

Lionel de Rothschild was elected by the City three more times; after each of them he took the oath on the Old Testament, and each time he was barred from taking his seat. But in 1853 the House of Commons passed a bill empowering each House to decide on its own form of oath. The Lords rejected this at first, but in 1858 they at last agreed, and the Commons omitted 'on the true faith of a Christian' from the oath. Seven years later the Lords did so too, thus enabling Jews to sit in the Upper House as well. But it was not until 1885 that a Jew actually did so, when Lionel de Rothschild's son Nathaniel was raised to the peerage by Queen Victoria.

The last restriction on Jews was removed in 1871, when an Act of Parliament enabled Jews to hold any office of State. In the same year Sir George Jessel became the first Jew to hold a ministerial post, when he was appointed Solicitor-General.

These disabilities and their removal naturally only affected a handful of Jews directly. The majority of the Jewish community had no ambitions to stand for Parliament or to hold high office. They were pleased, of course, every time a restriction was removed, and proud whenever a Jew attained distinction. But most of them had their hands full enough with making a living.

The early arrivals, the Sephardi Jews, were proud free men, culturally rich both in Jewish and worldly affairs. They came with wealth, prestige and quite often, high connections. Those who followed from the ghettoes of Germany, with a very few exceptions, had none of these advantages. They were well versed in Jewish learning, but the sciences and arts of the outside world were mostly closed books to them. They came with very few worldly goods, rich only in sad memories of past sufferings and in hopes for the future.

While the Sephardim shone as important merchants and brokers, the Ashkenazim (Hebrew for 'Germans', as Sephardim is Hebrew for 'Spaniards') were caricatured in British society as pedlars and second-hand clothes dealers, which were their main occupations.

The resulting distance which the Sephardi community set up between itself and the Ashkenazim was not praiseworthy but understandable, given the social conditions and snobberies of the time. The Ashkenazim were excluded from the charitable institutions and schools which the Sephardim had established, and even from the beautiful synagogue which they had built in the City of London. Even in matters affecting the Jewish community in their contacts with the outside world, the Sephardim kept themselves aloof, debarring the Ashkenazim from the Board of Deputies which they had set up to represent them. It was not until 1760 that the two communities combined — to congratulate George III on his accession to the throne. After that the Board of Deputies of British Jews, representing both communities, was formed.

However, the Ashkenazim gradually settled down in their new country, and spread out to the provinces. It was not long before they were able to build up their own welfare organization, their own synagogues and schools. With ever more and more new arrivals the Ashkenazim outgrew the Sephardim in numbers, and gradually even in economic standing.

They continued as separate communities, and remain so to this day. But the old animosity gradually diminished to vanishing point, and to all intents and purposes, apart from name, they may be said to have become one community, at least in matters affecting their relations with the outside world.

By the middle of the 19th century the Jews in Britain had well-established communal institutions, and since 1841 even their own periodical, the *Jewish Chronicle*, has been going strong to this day. They were thus able to cope with the crisis of the mass immigration at the end of the 19th century and the beginning of the 20th, of destitute Jews flying from the terror of the pogroms of Czarist Russia.

History repeated itself. The British Jews, Sephardim and Ashkenazim, were well-established and comparatively well off, and had adapted to the British way of life. The newcomers were penniless, Yiddish-speaking, and altogether 'foreign', even in their clothes. But this time the British Jews did everything they could to help the refugees. Those who wanted to go on farther west to America were helped with their passage expenses. Those who wanted to stay were helped both with relief and with employment.

Most of the refugees settled in the East End of London, where the Jewish population trebled within 20 years from 47,000. Others left for the provinces, to any place where a Jewish community already existed. They specialised in the production of cheap clothing, boots, furniture, and cigarettes. Israel Zangwill (1864-1926), the first novelist of the Jewish scene to attain an international reputation, immortalised the way of life of these Jewish refugees in their new home in his *Children*

Great Britain

of the Ghetto. But it was not long before the new arrivals settled into the British way of life, making great contributions to British economy, art and science.

The most recent mass influx of Jewish refugees into Britain was during the Nineteen Thirties, after the Nazis came to power in Germany. This time, however, the new immigrants were mostly well equipped with scientific, artistic, organisational or business experience. Nor, on the whole, were they penniless. Those who were, were generously assisted by a special fund opened for them by the British Jewish community. After a short time these newcomers were able to adjust to the new way of life and to make their full contribution to it.

All in all, the 300-year-old Jewish community in Britain has enjoyed a life free from persecution, and for the past hundred years has been unrestricted in activity, at liberty to enter any profession or calling. British Jews have made their mark in every walk of life, and have gone a very long way from the days when a Jew could not sit in Parliament. There have been very few governments in Britain in this century, Conservative, Liberal or Labour, which did not include a Jewish Minister.

But it would be an exaggeration to say that anti-Jewish prejudice has vanished from the British scene. There was open anti-semitism in many quarters after the mass arrival of the refugees at the end of the last century and the beginning of this one. There was the short-lived Fascist movement of the Nineteen-Thirties. There were also anti-Jewish riots after World War II, in the wake of Jewish terrorist activities against the British in Palestine. And there are still clubs where Jews are not wanted. It would probably be too much to expect that the centuries-old anti-Jewish prejudices could be eradicated completely in such a short time.

EPILOGUE

THE JEWISH STORY IS NOT ENDED. AFTER NEARLY two thousand years of exile the Jews—many of them—have returned to their ancient starting point, Israel. They are proud of their achievements there and in other lands.

But evil has not disappeared from the world. Justice and peace are goals still to be won. In some countries still, the Jews wait for deliverance. Even the newborn Jewish nation is beset by enemies. So the Jews go on praying for peace and justice and brotherhood for all men, for another giant step forward in man's long progress.

The Jews, it is often said, have stood at the gravesides

of all their persecutors. But this does not go far enough. Perhaps nations are the fuel of the civilisations which their geniuses create. The Jews had their message, the message of monotheism and social justice, and it has swept them on and on, consuming them in the process. But always, where civilisation has spread, in the mediaeval empires, in the Arab conquest, in the rise of Western Europe, in the New World, they were there, consumed by something they had helped to make themselves, and yet arising once again from the ashes. A tiny flame, but enough to carry on.

SUGGESTED READING LIST

The Six Day War by Randolph S. and Winston S. Churchill, Heinemann and Penguin, 1967

My People: A *History of the Jews* by Abba Eban, Weidenfeld and Nicolson, 1968

Anne Frank's Diary, Vallentine, Mitchell, Fifth Impression, 1973

The Popular Jewish Encyclopaedia by Rabbi Ben Isaacson and Deborah Wigoder, Vallentine, Mitchell, 1973

The Voices of Masada by David Kossoff, Vallentine, Mitchell, 1973

History of the Jewish People by James Parkes, Penguin, 1964

A *Short History of the Jewish People* by Cecil Roth, East and West Library, 1970

The Dreyfus Affair by Betty Schechter, Gollancz, 1965

The Encyclopaedia Judaica Editor-in-Chief: Cecil Roth. Available through Vallentine, Mitchell.

INDEX

Abraham, 12-13, 15, 25, 54, 188
Aelia Capitolina, 52, 60
Akiba, Rabbi, 51-52
Alexander II, Czar, 137
Almoravides, 86-87
American Jewish Congress, 182
Amsterdam, Holland, 121-122, 175
Apostles (disciples), 12, 41, 58-60
'Aqaba, Gulf of, 20, 26, 56, 196-199
Arabia and Arabs, 12, 40, 73-81, 82-84, 86-87, 90-91, 92, 163, 167, 182, 183, 184-190, 192-196, 200-201, 204, 206-208
Arabic, 74, 84
Aryans, 145, 170-171, 174
Assimilation, 155-158, 160, 164

Assyria, 27-28
Atonement, Day of (*Yom Kippur*), 14, 36, 75, 187
Austria, 135, 165, 181
Autos-da-fé, 108-109, 210-211

Babylonia (*See also* Mesopotamia), 28-29, 31-33, 56, 66, 67, 69, 82, 90, 195
Balfour Declaration, 180-181, 184, 185-187, 190
Balfour, Lord, 182, 185-186
Ballin, Albert, 130
Baptism, 103, 107-109, 112, 113-114, 115-116, 117, 120, 126-127, 136, 156, 158, 164, 176
Bar Giora, Simon, 47-48
Bar Kochba, Simon, 51-52, 55
Belgium, 177
Ben Eliezer, Israel, 151-152

Ben-Gurion, David, 194
Ben Hanania, Joshua, 64
Ben Israel, Menasseh, 122-123
Benjamin, Tribe of, 23, 26-27, 56
Ben Mattathias, Joseph, *See* Josephus, Flavius
Ben Zakkai, Rabbi Yohanan, 53-54
Bethlehem, 24, 38
Bible, 11, 13, 17, 21, 26, 31, 32, 33, 40, 78, 89, 91, 180
Black Death of 1348, 99, 201
Bonaparte, Napoleon, *See* Napoleon
Britain. *See* England and English
Buber, Martin, 155
Byzantium and Byzantines, 69-70, 73-74, 77-78, 80, 84, 182-183

· 229 ·

Cabala and Cabalists, 118, 150, 183
Cahena, Diah, 78-79, 82
Caliphs, 76, 90
Canaan, 12, 15, 18, 20-22, 25-26
Caro, Rabbi Joseph, 150-151
Casimir the Great, 104, 132
Castile, 106, 107, 109
Christ, *See* Jesus
Christianity and Christians, 12, 14, 32, 40, 57, 58-62, 63-64, 66, 68, 70, 73-74, 77, 78-79, 80, 81, 82, 83, 84, 85, 86-87, 88, 92-95, 98-99, 101, 103-104, 106-108, 110, 113, 116, 120-121, 122, 123, 125-127, 128, 133-134, 135, 136-138, 140, 141-142, 144, 149, 156-157, 159, 162, 166, 171, 174-175, 182, 183, 190, 203, 208, 210, 212
Christians, New, 107-114, 120-121, 124, 210
Columbus, 110-111, 209-210
Constantine the Great, Emperor, 61, 70
Constantinople, 78, 84, 115-116
Cossacks, 133-134
Crémieux, Adolphe, 130
Cromwell, Oliver, 123-124
Crusades and Crusaders, 88, 94-97, 106, 125, 126, 163, 173, 182, 193-194
Cyprus, 51
Cyrus, 32, 66, 195

David, 24-25, 26, 67, 194
Dead Sea (Salt Sea), 22, 40, 45
Dead Sea Scrolls, 40
Deborah, 23
Denmark, 175
Diaspora, 160-161, 202, 205-206

Disciples, *See* Apostles
Disraeli, Benjamin, 128
Dreyfus, Alfred, 146-147, 165, 170

Edward I, 102
Egypt and Egyptians, 15-18, 22, 28-29, 45-46, 51, 56, 77-78, 89, 138, 185, 191, 195, 196-201
Ehrlich, Paul, 130
Eilat, Israel, 196
Einstein, Albert, 131
Eleazar, 47-48
England (Britain) and English, 27, 51, 56 88, 96-97, 102-103, 123-124, 127-128, 129-130, 138, 140-141, 143, 156, 158, 159, 164, 167, 175, 177, 180-190, 191, 197, 204, 211, 212
Espinoza, Baruch (Benedict) d', *See* Spinoza
Euphrates river, 12
Exilarch, 67, 71, 90

Faith, Thirteen Articles of, 89
Ferdinand of Aragon, 109-110, 113, 115, 122, 209
"Final solution," 147, 202
Florus, 44-45
France and French, 79, 81, 95-96, 98, 103, 121, 125-126, 128, 129, 130, 140, 145-147, 156, 165, 170-171, 177, 183-184, 185, 197, 211
Franco-Prussian War, 145, 170
Freud, Sigmund, 130

Galilee and Galileans, 21-22, 40, 44, 46-48, 55, 117, 163, 171
Gaza Strip, 196-198
Gemara, See Talmud and Talmudists

Gentiles, 60, 105, 141-142, 144, 159, 165, 175, 182, 203, 212, 213, 214
Germany and Germans, 62, 96, 98, 103-104, 110, 121, 124, 126-127, 129, 130, 135, 140, 143, 146, 156, 157, 158, 159, 161, 170-177, 178-179, 181, 188, 203
Ghetto, 126, 142, 158, 159, 167, 176, 213
Gobineau, Count Joseph Arthur de, 145, 170
God, one, 13, 19, 59, 72, 74-75, 78, 149
Golan Heights, 199
Goliath, 24
Greece and Greeks, 34, 38, 56, 66, 73, 77, 115, 116, 177

Hadrian, Emperor, 51-52, 59
Haffkine, Waldemar, 130
Hannukah, feast of, 34-35
Hassidim, 151-155
Hebrew language, 11-12, 31, 35, 53, 55, 66, 69, 84, 85, 91, 101, 105, 115, 141, 150, 157, 207
Heine, Heinrich, 127
Hejaz, the (Saudi Arabia), 185-187
Henry VIII, 141
Herod the Great, King, 38-39, 45-46, 56
Herzl, Theodor, 165-168
Hillel, Rabbi, 36
Hitler, Adolf, 62, 147, 169, 173-175, 177, 188-189, 202, 214
Holland (the Netherlands) and Dutch, 116, 121-124, 126, 131, 161, 175, 177, 211
Holy Roman Empire, 84, 119
Hungary, 156, 165

Index

India, 27, 70, 129-130, 186, 188, 194
Indians, American, 123, 211
Industrial Revolution, 128
Inquisition, Mexican, 210-211
Inquisition, Portuguese, 108-109, 113-114, 119, 120-121, 156
Inquisition, Spanish, 108-109, 113-114, 120-121, 156, 210
Iraq, 12, 29, 73, 185-186, 191-192, 195, 207
Isaac, 13, 188
Isabella of Castile, 109-110, 113, 122
Islam and Moslems. 12, 14, 32, 75-81, 83, 84, 86-87, 88, 89, 90, 91, 95, 106, 107, 109, 110, 115, 149, 156, 162, 163, 167, 183, 184-185, 186, 187-188, 190, 195
Israel and Israelis. 20, 24, 26-27, 137, 149, 161, 180, 191-201, 202, 204-208
Italy and Italians, 112, 121, 127, 129

Jacobi, Moritz, 131
Jacob-Israel, 11, 15, 188
Jeremiah, 31-32, 54
Jerusalem, 24-25, 27, 29, 30-34, 37, 38, 43, 44-45, 47-49, 50, 51, 52, 53, 60, 66-67, 76, 92, 95, 102, 105, 126, 160, 161, 184-185, 187, 188, 193-194, 195, 199-200
Jerusalem, Temple of, 25-26, 29, 30-34, 38, 44-45, 49-50, 51, 52, 53-54, 55-56, 66-67, 73, 102, 148, 149, 159, 187-188, 195, 205-206
Jessel, Sir George, 127-128
Jesus (Christ), 12, 14, 38-42, 56, 58, 59, 60-61, 64, 73, 95-99, 121, 123, 133-135, 138, 141, 159, 171, 173, 203
Jewish State, The, 166
John of Gishala, 47-48
John the Baptist, 40
Jordan, 20, 73, 193, 196, 197-199, 200-201
Jordan River, 187, 190, 193, 199, 201
Josephus, Flavius (Joseph ben Mattathias), 47-49, 51
Joshua, 22, 46
Judah, Tribe and Kingdom of, 11, 20, 24, 26-28, 30, 56
Judea, 20, 34, 37-40, 42, 44-46, 48, 50, 51-52, 102, 183, 191

Karaites, 69
Khazars, 79-81, 82
Kohanim family, 31, 78-79
Koran, 75

"Ladino." 110-111
Latin, 50, 83-84, 126
Law of Return, 194
League of Nations 180, 183, 185, 188-189, 190
Lebanon, 20, 185, 191, 195
Levi, Tribe of, 25
Libya, 51
Lippman, Gabriel, 131
"Lost Tribes," 27, 123

Maccabee family, 34-35, 38
Maimonides, 88-89, 203
Marcus, Siegfried, 131
Marranos, 107-108, 114, 118, 120-121, 122, 124-125, 161, 210-211
Marx, Karl, 158
Mar Zutra II, 71
Masada, 45-46, 50-51, 198
"Master race," 171-173, 176, 178, 214
Mecca, 74-76

Meir, Golda, 137, 182
Melchett, Lord, 130
Mellah, 167
Menasseh, *See* ben Israel, Menasseh
Mendelssohn, Moses, 157-158
Mesopotamia (*See also* Babylonia), 66-71, 77-78, 80, 85, 90, 185
Messiah, 39, 42, 60-61, 64, 89, 101, 118, 123, 141, 161, 162-164, 179, 182, 206
Messiahs, false, 118-119, 161-162, 173, 178
Miguez, Joao, *See* Nasi, Joseph
Mishnah, 55, 65, 69
Mohammed, 12, 74-79, 87
Molcho, Solomon (Diogo Pires), 118-119
Mond, Ludwig, 130
Moses, 16-19, 21
Moslems, *See* Islam and Moslems
Mufti, 185, 187

Napoleon, 125-126, 145
Nasi, Joseph (Joao Miguez), 116-118, 164
Nationalism, 42, 140-141, 143-144, 164
Nazis, 110, 173-177, 179, 192, 202, 205, 213, 214
Nebuchadnezzar, 28-29, 32-33, 49, 66, 73
Netherlands, the, *See* Holland and Dutch
New Testament, 58, 61, 139
Nicholas I, Czar, 136
North Africa, 86-88, 89, 91, 111, 167

Ochs, Adolph, 130
Old Testament, 17-18, 60-61, 65, 69, 139-140, 143
Orthodox Jews, 166

"Pale of Jewish Settlement," the, 136-137
Palestine (Palaestina) and Palestinians, 12, 20, 52, 55-56, 58, 63, 64, 66, 68, 74, 78, 90-91, 97, 101, 116-118, 141, 150, 159, 160-161, 163-168, 179-190, 191-193
Passover, 16-17, 31, 97, 125, 140, 161
Patriarchate, 54-55, 64, 68
Paul, 58-59
Pentecost, 31
Persia and Persians, 32, 66, 69-71, 77-78, 163, 167, 183
Pharisees, 35-37, 41, 58, 60
Philistines, 22-24, 25-26, 52, 176
Phoenicians, 23, 26
Pires, Diogo, See Molcho, Solomon
Pogrom, 137-138, 164
Poland and Polish, 104, 132-136, 149-150, 151-152, 154, 161, 175, 176-177, 181, 208
Pompey, 37
Pontius Pilate, 43-44
Portugal and Portuguese, 108-109, 111, 112-114, 115-116, 117, 118, 120, 122, 124, 136, 161, 211
Prepared Table, The, 150-151
Prophets, 24, 26, 31, 39, 54, 59, 60, 161, 173, 194
Psalms, 24-25, 31

Rabbis, 33-37, 40-41, 51-52, 53-55, 64-66, 68-69, 90, 96, 105, 117, 118, 122, 148-151, 155, 166, 179, 207
Red Sea, 17, 20, 22, 56, 73, 74
Reform Judaism, 158-159, 160, 166

Rehoboam, 26
Renaissance, 121
Reuter, Paul, 130
Revolution, French, 125, 147
Rome, Roman Empire and Romans, 19, 37, 38-39, 41-42, 43-52, 54-55, 56, 57, 60, 61-62, 66, 67, 69-70, 73, 92-93, 118-119, 126, 127, 140, 141, 142, 160-161, 163
Rothschild family, 127, 129-130
Russia and Russians, 56, 105, 133-138, 156, 164, 167, 176-177, 178, 183-184, 196, 200, 204, 207-208

Sabbath, 19, 34, 36, 41, 57, 59, 61, 65, 70, 86, 108, 149, 153-154
Sacrifices, 13-14, 25, 32, 33, 34, 45, 54
Sadducees, 35-37, 41, 69
Safed, Palestine, 150, 183
Samaritans, 28, 32-33, 69
Samson, 23, 176, 205
Samuel, 23-24, 26
Sanhedrin, 53-55, 117
Saudi Arabia, See Hejaz, the
Saul, 23-24
Schwarz, David, 131
Shabbetai Zevi, 161-162
Shofar, 187
Sinai desert, 18, 20
Sinai Peninsula, 16, 17, 167, 196-198
Sinai War of 1956, 197
Six-day war, 198
Solomon, 25-26, 29, 49, 56
Spain and Spanish, 79, 82-89, 91, 92, 106-111, 112, 113-114, 116, 117, 120, 124, 131, 136, 150, 161, 175, 203, 209, 210

Spinoza (Baruch [Benedict] d'Espinoza), 121-122
Suez Canal, 17, 129-130, 181-182, 196, 197, 199, 201
Sweden, 175
Switzerland, 128, 166, 175
Synagogues, 32, 33, 35, 57, 80, 101, 142, 149, 161 194, 211, 212
Syria and Syrians, 20, 25-26, 34, 37, 38, 46-47, 56, 74, 77-78, 185, 188, 191, 195, 197-199, 207

Tabernacles, Feast of, 31, 37
Talmud and Talmudists, 66, 68-69, 85, 91, 93, 148-149, 150, 151, 153, 155-157, 188, 209
Ten Commandments, 18-19, 41
Theodosius II, Emperor, 62
Tiberias, Palestine, 91, 117, 164
Titus, 47-50, 53, 191
Torah, 31-32, 33-34
Transjordan, 187, 191, 193
Treitschke, Heinrich von, 171-172, 174
Tribes, ancient Jewish, 11, 23, 24, 25, 26-27, 56, 123
Turkey, Turkish Empire and Turks, 115-116, 134, 150, 161-162, 163, 166-167, 175, 181, 182, 183-184, 185

United Nations, (U.N.), 180, 190, 191-193, 197-198, 200-201, 204
United States, (U.S.), 105, 128, 138, 144, 158, 164, 172, 177, 181, 193, 197, 199, 212-214

Index

Vespasian, 47-48, 50
Vogel, Sir Julius, 130

"Wailing Wall," (Western Wall), 52, 187, 194, 200
Warsaw, Poland, 176
Weizmann, Dr. Chaim, 167, 181, 185-186, 194
Western Wall, *see* "Wailing Wall"

White Paper, British, 189
World War I, 172, 181
World War II, 175-177, 178, 189, 202

Yathrib, 75, 76
Yemen, 73-74, 167, 194-195
Yiddish, 104-105, 207
Yom Kippur, *See* Atonement, Day of

Yugoslavia, 177

Zadik, 152-155
Zevi, Shabbetai, *See* Shabbetai Zevi
Zionism, 160-168, 180-181, 186, 204
Zionist Organization, 180
Zola, Emile, 146
Zoroastrianism, 70